Your Financial Freedom

Through Network Marketing

Distribution:

For Canada:

Les éditions Un monde différent ltée
3925 Grande-Allée
Saint-Hubert (Québec)
Canada J4T 2V8
Tél.: (514) 656-2660
Fax.: (514) 445-9098

This book is translated from French to English, Italian, Spanish, Portuguese, Polish, Dutch.

Second printing, Revised edition, September 1994

Cover graphic design: SERGE HUDON

With the cooperation of: ALINE LÉVESQUE

Phototypesetting and formatting: COMPOSITION MONIKA, QUÉBEC

ISBN: 2-89225-088-9

(French edition: ISBN 2-89225-189-3; Spanish edition: ISBN 2-89225-5229-6; Portuguese edition: ISBN 2-89225-212-1; Polish edition: ISBN 83-900946-1-4)

Your
Financial
Freedom

Through
Network
Marketing

André Blanchard

Les éditions Un monde différent ltée 3925
Grande-Allée St. Hubert, Quebec Canada J4T 2V8 Tel:
(514) 656-2660 Fax: (514) 445-9098

To a wonderful woman, my best friend, Françoise.

The woman with whom and for whom I have been building this business for more than 28 years.

Table of contents

PART ONE: AN OVERVIEW   13

     Foreword   15

Chapter 1: The ideal business   19

     The system of the future   21

     Free enterprise   22

Chapter 2: Introduction to network marketing   25

     Its definition   25

     Network marketing and pyramidal sales schemes.   25

     Its main characteristics   26

     — The theory of leverage.   27

     — The network principle.   28

     The success of network marketing is equal to the quality of its components. .   28

     Who should we associate with?   28

     a) The Company: criteria for selecting the best   28

- The owners 30
- Is the company financially sound?.. 30
- A code of commercial ethics........ 30
- Longevity........................... 31
- Mandatory inventory 31
- Representation 31
- The legacy 31
- b) The sponsor and the associates 31

The competition 33

The real recipe?...................... 34

Ambition 35

The vision 36

What is your vision? 38

PART TWO: MOTIVATION 43

Chapter 3: The Rolls Royce of network marketing!............................ 45

The Amway Environment Foundation . 49

Press kit

Souvenir album: 28 years

Chapter 4: A dream lifestyle!............ 51

What you are looking for is looking for you................................... 51

A first hurdle........................ 53

A second hurdle 54

A simple start 56

Three months later.................. 58

A smashing success 59

A resounding success 61

Beyond all expectations 62

Economic repercussions 64

An active participation 64

A philosophy of life 65

Growing in the business world 66

From generation to generation 68

Leisure 70

Aim high 71

Dreams and more dreams! 71

Smell the roses 72

Beyond the tangible 72

Our values 73

Life is a bank account 74

A balance in life 74

A second nature 75

When you have a problem: do
something about it 77

**Chapter 5: Be convinced and you will be
convincing** 79

Convince through emotions 79

The last laugh! 80

Sweet revenge 81

Tell me who your friends are 82

Be convinced of the benefits of network
marketing 82

Proof at hand. 83

A living proof 84

A winning attitude. 85

PART THREE: THE SUCCESS SYSTEM . . 87

Chapter 6: How to build an organization . . 89

A) The importance of the success
    system. 89

How to help someone develop his
network 90

1. Assess your associate 90

Profile of leaders. 91

The 20/80 law 92

2. Teach them the ABC's of the perfect
    distributor 93

B) Merchandising 94

1. Distribution 94
    a) Consuming or using your
       products 94
    b) Retail and wholesale distribution 95

2. Duplication 97
    a) Support. 98
    b) Quitters. 99

C) Make it stick together 99

Chapter 7: The commandments for success 103

The burning desire. 103

My recipe 106

A fool-proof method 107

Basics you must do 107

How attitude affects your success 113

Devote your life 118

Always think big 119

Chapter 8: Two invitations 121

An invitation to never quit........... 121

A personal invitation................ 125

To risk........................... 126

Glossary 127

Part one:

An Overview

Foreword

It is 7 a.m. and 28 °C. I slowly sip my champagne and orange juice as the soft breeze gently caresses my face. I am sitting on the top deck of the Sea Goddess I, a Cunard luxury liner, cruising the Mediterranean from Rome to Sorrento.

I sit back, day-dreaming and recalling all the work and efforts of the past 28 years: the rewards, the goals achieved and the ones that had to wait, the new friendships, the trips we made, the luxurious lifestyle my family and I have enjoyed, a life free of conventional routines and budgets, and occasionally, a life filled with adventure.

Thousands of images come to my mind: sceneries, faces, emotional moments, victories, defeats, laughters, tears, ups, downs, competitors, scavengers, winners, friendships. All shoot through my mind in sequence, bringing back a world of memories.

I see myself back at the beginning of this great adventure, a timid inexperienced novice, with few or no dreams, and no specific goals in mind, joining a large organization, not knowing where it would lead me.

I compare that to the man sitting here today, a veteran world traveller, forever thankful for the abundance of riches that life has bestowed upon us, and the attitude I have developed. Back in 1967, in my wildest dreams, I could not begin to see myself as I am now. First of all, it would have required that I sit down and admit that such possibilities even existed. In those days, even the world's greatest fortune teller could not have convinced me that I would change so dramatically.

I could never have pictured myself with the people I am associated with today, the friends I have made, or the lifestyle that this business opportunity has allowed me to live. And yet, it is this very philosophy and this lifestyle that has enabled me to face life's responsibilities and challenges.

I always knew it took hard work to earn a living but when I came across this opportunity and began to earn a living through network marketing, I realized that life can bring tremendous rewards that oftentimes go far beyond anything one dares to imagine.

As this peaceful cruise on the quiet waters of the Italian Riviera comes to an end at the port of Sorrento, the sound of the sailors preparing to dock interrupts my reverie, and my thoughts return to today, 28 years after the great adventure began.

And it was, at this precise moment that a realization quickly came to my mind; all the rewards that my wife and I received were well worth the efforts we had invested in this great business. Convinced by this thought, I eagerly renewed my personal commitment to my network marketing business. At that moment, in that frame of mind I decided to share our lifetime experiences with you, hoping that what we have accomplished will help you to realize the unlimited potential that network marketing has to offer.

The ship has now docked. Sorrento awaits us. The dream continues to unfold.

Free Enterprise

Excerpt from a declaration by Abraham Lincoln,
President of the United States, to the Congress in 1860

You cannot

- *create prosperity by discouraging savings;*
- *give strength to the weak by weakening the strong;*
- *help the worker by destroying the employer;*
- *favour brotherhood of man by encouraging the war between the classes;*
- *help the poor by ruining the rich;*
- *avoid problems by spending more than you earn;*
- *shape character and courage by discouraging initiative and independence;*
- *continually help man by doing for him what he can do for himself.*

Chapter 1

The Ideal Business

The vast experience I have gained during my 28 years of professional life makes it possible for me to take the next few pages to introduce you to the world's simplest form of business, a concept that I believe is the blueprint for the "ideal" business.

It is as simple as saying "hello". However, simple is not always easy. But then, does anything which comes easy has any real value?

First, we must define the "ideal" business. The eleven criteria set forth below provide a clear definition for "the ideal business".

"There never was a perfect business, and there never will be. However, let's assume that any business exists to produce profits. I have long pondered on the various factors which might combine to produce the perfect business.

Feel free to use this list to evaluate your present profession or the company for which you now work, or simply to compare two different businesses or, you may want to use this list as a reference to measure the potential for a new enterprise.

1) The ideal business sells to the entire world, rather than a single neighbourhood or a single city or locality (in other words, it has a huge market).

2) The ideal business has a product with "constant demand". This means that people need it regardless of price.

3) The ideal business has low labour requirements; the fewer people needed, the better.

4) The ideal business sells a product which fits a continuing human (or animal) need. It's not a fad product, it's not a product which people can easily substitute or even do without.

5) The ideal business has low overhead: it does not need an expensive location, it does not need large amounts of utilities, advertising, legal advice, etc.

6) The ideal business produces a product which is difficult (or almost impossible) for a competitor to copy or reproduce. This means the product is unique (such as a publication), or it is designed for a specific consumption, or it is a product which is protected by copyright or patent.

7) The ideal business does not require huge cash expenditures or large investments in equipment. In other words, it does not tie up your money.

8) The ideal business is a business that has continuous cash flow; your money is not tied up in extended credit arrangements.

9) The ideal business is relatively free from all kinds of government and industry regulations.

10) The ideal business is portable. You can take it anywhere you go.

11) Here's a crucial but overlooked one: the ideal business is one that remains exciting, even when it tends to stretch your intellectual and often your emotional capabilities.

There you are. If you use this list, it might help you cut through a lot of nonsense and hypocrisy about what you are doing and what you are looking for. None of us work for or own an ideal business. But it's nice to know what one would consist of*.

In my opinion, network marketing is the closest thing to the ideal business.

The system of the future

More and more, within the business world, we are hearing statements that corroborate that network marketing is the system of the future.

At the present time, many business people have earned a great deal of money through network marketing.

The current trend indicates that 50 % to 60 % of all products and services will be sold through network marketing during the next decade. Educators and economists alike agree that network marketing is here to stay.

---

* Source: Dow Theory Letters Inc. Summer 1984.

Why is this system so promising? The answer is simple. The concept is based on cooperation, a notion that makes it possible for an unlimited amount of people to share products and services through an exceptional method known as network marketing.

Experts in the business field all over the world support the fact that within the next five years network marketing will be the new way to purchase goods and services.

Free enterprise

The backbone of the free enterprise system is the independent business person and network marketing is free enterprise in its purest form.

Network marketing, undoubtedly the most exciting and lucrative business concept in the history of the world, appeals to both the individual and entrepreneur alike and many of them decide to convert their present business to this method of distribution.

Gerald Ford, former President of the United States once said during a conference: "The thousands of Amway distributors are living proof that free enterprise is, and will continue to be, a vibrant force both at home, and around the world."

"Network marketing is digging a well before being thirsty.

When one becomes thirsty, one may not have the strength to dig."

Chapter 2

Introduction to Network Marketing

Its definition

For the last few years, the expression "networking" has become a staple in the business jargon. This expression is defined as the art of making and using contacts.

In fact, network marketing is the merchandising of products and/or services of a business or businesses through a network, created by virtue of contacts and referrals and which operates through the entrepreneurship of each of the people involved.

Network marketing versus pyramidal schemes

At this point, it is important to clear up any confusion that may exist between the concept of network marketing and that of pyramidal sales, an illegal system which makes it possible for only a few people to profit from a large number of consumers.

In the 70's, network marketing and pyramidal sales were falsely regarded as similar businesses. Let us begin by recreating the context.

Pyramidal sales companies (Koscot, Holiday Magic, CarBar, etc.) were operating on a fraudulent basis: the founding members were the ones and only true beneficiaries as the pyramid expanded, hence the name pyramidal system (the people at the top of the pyramid would reap all the benefits).

Many poor souls who were searching for a dream actually purchased a nightmare.

In a legitimate business like network marketing, you may earn more than your sponsor, even if you join his group years later. You can also earn more than any of your predecessors.

Its main characteristics

Network marketing is a simple business. This does not necessarily mean that it is easy. It is simply a method that allows a product or service to be distributed to the consumer almost directly from the manufacturer.

In a traditional business, the manufacturer sells his products to a broker or a factory rep, who sells to a wholesaler, who in turn sells them to the retailer, who sells to the consumer.

M⇒   B⇒   W⇒   R⇒   C

Manufacturer Broker Wholesaler Retailer Consumer

Each intermediary must pay his staff, cover his overhead and make a profit. Furthermore, selling the product requires large sums of money to be invested in advertising through newspapers, radio, television, mail, etc.

Therefore, the product must be sold at a high and sometimes outrageous price, in order for everyone to make a profit and cover advertising costs.

Network marketing simplifies the process: the manufacturer sells directly to the distributor who also consumes and distributes their own goods and services.

M⇒   D/C

Manufacturer Distributor/Consumer

This method eliminates many intermediaries and the manufacturer does not have to spend a fortune in advertising costs. The money saved is redistributed to all the distributors ready to invest their time and efforts to raise the customer's awareness about their products.

This type of business requires that you constantly focus your energy on two areas:

1. Personally use your products and services.

2. Sponsor individuals who will also use, distribute, sponsor and so on. It is the effective application of the principle of duplication.

The theory of leverage

In real estate, many people have built their fortune by applying the leverage theory to their real estate values.

In our business, we learn to leverage our time whereby if we have five or ten available hours a week and we sponsor tens and eventually hundreds of individuals in our network, who in turn do the same thing, we will achieve the results produced by hundreds or thousands of hours of productive work. It really is duplication in action.

The network principle

As the name implies, network marketing bases its development on the creation of a viable network of people.

In order to achieve optimum results, a good climate should be present to merchandise the products and services and to devote the necessary energy to build a network.

Therefore, it is important that each component of your network is of the highest quality. In order to ensure the best possible results, it is imperative that you be very selective in your choice of the following three components:

1) the parent company you will be dealing with
2) your sponsor
3) your future distributors or associates.

The success of the network is equal to the quality of its components

WHO SHOULD WE ASSOCIATE WITH?

a)   The company: criteria for selecting the best

It is very important to associate yourself with a company that shows a great deal of stability, ethics, longevity and long term profitability.

Beware of new companies, especially those that promise you the moon. They usually last no longer than six months to a year. Oftentimes, you'll hear these claims: "It is new, it is the opportunity of a lifetime. It is just *like Amway*, but much better" or even "Join while it is new; it is a ground floor opportunity. Being first is a golden opportunity". You are shown the glitter of being the first and led to believe that this translates automatically into big money.

The opportunity to join such "ground floor" businesses most often turns to tragedy in this type of concept. The problem with being first is that you may become last should the company phase out. It is an undisputed fact that in 28 years, I have seen tens if not hundreds of companies venture into network marketing. Very few have survived. The others have simply disappeared for many reasons.

Oftentimes, their demise was the result of continually changing their sales plan when the company was facing financial difficulties. Low quality products can destroy a business. Inadequate financing by the founders has doomed many a network marketing business. Another reason which is rarely mentioned but is nonetheless a very important factor is the lack of integrity of its management.

These companies try to use the popularity of the network marketing concept to develop their network, taking advantage of the enormous wave created by giants such as Amway, Shaklee and Mary Kay Ash, who have turned out to be the pillars of this industry.

Those countless failures of the past stress the importance of carefully assessing your future parent company.

Information on the company

Before you take the important decision to join a network marketing organization, carefully verify the following aspects of the company you are considering dealing with.

The owners

Who are the owners? Do they have any experience in the field?

Is the company publicly or privately owned? This can be an important factor in the decision making process. The shareholders sometimes sacrifice quality for the sake of profits.

Is the company financially sound?

Look for a company that has an excellent reputation, preferably one that has no debts. There is a limit to the bonuses a company can hand out and its debt ratio can stop it from keeping its promises. Beware of companies that promise tons of dollars or a very large income for little effort.

A code of commercial ethics

Enquire about the business' code of ethics. See how the code is taught and then applied throughout the organization.

Does the company take on the responsibility of verifying its distributors' qualifications and of dismissing those who go against the company's and other distributors general policies?

Does the company offer a full buy-back agreement, minus a restocking fee, on products that were ordered but remained unsold?

Longevity

Find out in which year the company was established. It will give you the opportunity to analyze their past results, growth, credibility, etc., and find out if their concept has weathered the test of time.

Mandatory inventory

Think twice before joining a company that insists you purchase inventory to get started. This means that you must purchase a specific amount of their products in order to reach a level. In short, you are purchasing a title. In my many years in business, I have never seen one of these types of companies last very long.

Representation

Serious companies have an association of distributors, headed by a board of directors elected by those distributors. The company should also select experienced distributors to sit on committees for long term planning, future projects and challenges.

The legacy

Last but not least, ensure that your business will survive long after you are gone. You should be able to will the business to your legal heirs.

Would you seriously want to spend many years building a successful business only to have it return to the company at the time of your death? Make sure that you can pass on your business, or sell it, if you so desire.

b)   *The sponsor and your associates*

This business is based on mutual trust. You may sponsor a stranger, a friend or a member of your family but in order to develop belief, there should be a natural attraction between you and the people you sponsor; fraternal bonds should be established.

Sad, but true, it is a fact that a large majority of the people who quit this type of business, do so because of human personality conflicts and not because it is not lucrative.

There is another interesting element to consider. In a traditional business, you go into business, open your doors and wait for customers to come by your shop. You have no control over those with whom you do business. In network marketing, you have the liberty to choose the people you wish to associate and to work with.

Throughout my experience of many years in this business, I have come to realize that the people most interested in listening to this type of opportunity are those who are already living a successful life. It is becoming more obvious these days, that the people who join network marketing are not those who need more, but rather those who want more.

THE MORE A PERSON IS TRUSTWORTHY THE MORE HE/SHE GROWS. SPONSOR THE MOST PROSPEROUS AND THE MOST DYNAMIC PEOPLE YOU KNOW.

The competition

Competition helps us stay alert and competitive. Thanks to competition our service remains the best. Network marketing is on the threshold of a new era and many companies will choose this method to merchandise their products or services.

This is the main reason why industrial giants such as Kodak, Gerber, Philips, Coca-Cola, MCI, Grolier, etc. have selected the Amway network for the distribution of some of their products.

When a person decides to start with a network marketing company he or she should take the time to assess the different benefits that are offered.

Unfortunately, most people do not take the time to do this kind of research before joining a network marketing business. They listen to anyone who sounds impressive and full of promises when, in reality, these people represent new companies with little or no background.

In an American magazine, the Direct Selling Association recently suggested four factors to consider before joining a direct selling company. The potential salesperson must first examine:

1. the product line offered;

2.   the management;

3.   the marketing plan and the benefits it offers;

4.   the company's commitment towards quality training and assistance.

It is also important that all bonuses are paid on time, that the company manufactures its main products, and that it offers the opportunity to develop a network throughout the world.

In fact, one of the main characteristics that the ideal company should exhibit is that its primary objective is focused on the ever expanding growth of its distributor base and on the volume of products sold.

Beware of companies who promise rewards based solely on recruiting, or those who require you to purchase a wide inventory upon joining. They have nothing to lose. They will have had ample time to make enough money to start a new business if this one fails in order to appeal to the next group of hopeful individuals who want to make a fortune without working for it.

The real recipe?

Time after time, people have asked me during the last 28 years: "Is there one sure recipe for success in the network marketing field?"

I am also asked: "Can you profile a successful or ideal candidate for network marketing?" Each time, I am forced to answer that there is no such model and no such recipe. I have met thousands of people who have been successful in this business and all of them came from different backgrounds: the place they were born, the color of their skin, their education, their family environment, their profession, their religion, and their principles were of little importance. In appearance, there seemed no common denominator.

However, as time went by, I did realize and I do remain convinced that although not everyone will reach success as quickly as we did, that *anyone* who has vision and ambition can reach his/her full potential in this type of business.

Ambition

Perhaps sometimes you may be tempted to ask: "What is the use of being consumed with ambition if I do not have the education, the money, or a plan that will allow me to do something about it?"

The fact that you are reading this book is, I hope, a sign that you are ambitious and that you are looking for means to make your dreams come true.

In what possible field could a person with little education be allowed to make more money in one month than most people earn in one year? Network marketing is that field!

In which field are you allowed as a person with no money to make a fortune without investing a dime? Again, network marketing, of course!

In which field are you allowed to start a business and obtain all the information and all the secrets, from all the experts, at no cost? Network marketing, of course!

How long have you been searching for the ideal plan or business?

Developing a business through network marketing enables you to multiply the results of your efforts. By applying the leverage theory to your time, which all financial wizards preach about, you can create a duplication process that will give you the freedom you have always dreamed of.

J. Paul Getty, who was undoubtedly the richest man in the world at the time of his death, said that all you have to do to succeed is to manufacture consumable products which are used frequently by each and everyone of us, and to do so in a way that they become the best products at the best possible prices. Then you will surely become rich.

Here is yet another quote attributed to him:

"I would prefer to receive 1% on the results of the efforts of 100 people than 100% of my own efforts."

The vision

One of the most important things in life, and a must in my own life, is to have the freedom to do the things that I want to do, when and where I want to and with whom I want to, knowing that no one or nothing can stop me from doing it.

I have always wanted to live a life in that fashion. However, I was fully aware that one had to work hard before reaping the fruits of one's labour. I was ready to take on that challenge. I have never been afraid of hard work especially when it is the type of work I enjoy doing.

When the opportunity to join a network marketing business was presented to me, it was the answer to my prayers. I was obsessed by my childhood days. I vividly remembered all the suffering that my family and I had endured.

As a result of illness, my father became an invalid at the age of 35. He died ten years later leaving my mother penniless with 5 children, no insurance whatsoever and many debts. I was 12 at the time and I was forced to quit school and go to work. I promised myself then, that when I would have a family of my own, I would never make them go through what my family had experienced.

Hence, I was one of those candidates with no education or money who refused to live in mediocrity. I lived and hoped for success and had dreams of a better future. I fervently harbored that desire within.

What I call "the vision" is the ability to vividly visualize future results and to immediately put in all the necessary efforts required now, in order to one day reach that desired goal.

Medical students are an excellent example to illustrate this point. For many years, they put all their energies into learning and training, knowing well the kind of life they will live six or seven years down the road. This is also true of those who have the potential of an entrepreneur. They are ready to invest time now because they expect results from their efforts in the future.

Network marketing was offering me the opportunity to one day have the security that I had lacked so much throughout my childhood that is, first the security, and then financial independence. Why not?

All I had to do was take the decision to build my future, to succeed "no matter what". The next step was to act, plus accept the fact that I would have to temporarily set aside certain leisure activities, and even people that could hold me back knowing that I would fully enjoy and appreciate them later.

These are choices one has to make for a better and bigger future. Personally, even though I was a devout hockey fan, I chose to eliminate this activity for a while. It was a wise choice, when you consider that the ones getting rich are the players, not the spectators. You may share my point of view now, but my friends at the time, did not understand at all.

What is your vision?

Why don't we evaluate your vision and imagination. Count the number of squares in the illustration that follows. How many do you see?

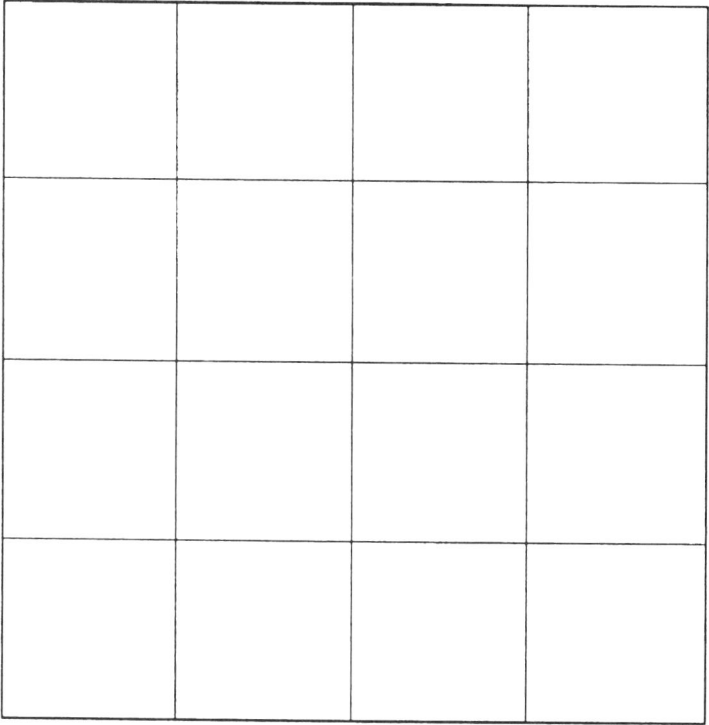

If you counted sixteen squares, you are part of the majority. If you counted 17, you have still missed some, but you are heading in the right direction.

Before checking for the answers, I invite you to stretch your imagination a bit more to try to see how many additional squares you can actually find.

1	2	3	4
5	6	7	8
9	10	11	12
13	14	15	16

You see, there are 30 squares.

Now let your imagination run wild. What if it was a cube? How many squares would you see then? Think about it.

Well done! Network marketing offers just as many unforeseen opportunities. Believe me, I have been seeing it happen for a long time.

Try to develop your own vision or what I call "the attitude" or the entrepreneur's mentality. Don't follow the masses who are slaves to their employee mentality all through their life. I constantly quote one of the first employers I worked for when I was 14 or 15 years old. "The smallest business is better than the biggest job, because *you* are the one who makes the decisions."

As a result of the meetings we attended, all the motivational tapes we have listened to and the self-help books we have read, Françoise and I both discovered that we were worth far more than what any employer was willing to pay us. We became conscious of our worth.

If you are starting out in network marketing or have been at it for a while but have not yet reached your goals, this book will undoubtedly answer your questions — or at least I hope it will. The information it contains will allow you to grasp the scope of the concept and will encourage you to act.

Unfortunately, I cannot guarantee that you will succeed. However, I will not claim glory for your success nor take part in your failure because it has been proven that the potential is there. Only YOU can decide to act. Place your bets! It will become easier to go ahead if you clearly dream of the lifestyle you want to live. WHY is much more important than HOW. When you'll know WHY, you'll be teachable.

Become a fanatic about your network marketing business. Sooner or later, the people who surround you will respect what you believe in.

Remove your blinders, roll up your sleeves and give it all you've got. Only YOU can do it.

Will you do it? Will you succeed? Your fate lies in your own hands!

"Give a person a fish, and he will feed on it for one day. Show him how to fish, and he will feed himself for life."

> *"Start doing what you can do, what you dream of doing. Audacity is a mixture of genius, power and magic."*
>
> Goethe

Part two:

Motivation

There is a line from an old song which says that love "makes the world go "round". At the risk of sounding hopelessly antiromantic, I would like to revise that line slightly: it is respect that makes the world go' round. The most important commodity in the world is respect for the individual man.

Richard DeVos and
Charles Paul Conn
in *Believe!*

Chapter 3

The Rolls Royce of Network Marketing!

Very few companies can meet this challenge. Unquestionably, the leader at the forefront of the entire networking industry has been and remains to be AMWAY. It is generally agreed that the company has done more, and continues to do more in furthering the development of the network marketing concept than any other company in history.

In the past, many people truly misunderstood what Amway was all about, mainly because of the way the information was presented to them.

The book entitled *The Possible Dream* by Charles Paul Conn, offers one of the best explanations about the true nature of the Amway Corporation.

"The dream of Rich DeVos and Jay Van Andel was to build a company that would offer anyone who wanted a chance to change their lives. Their dream was to offer those who would work for it a chance to build their own business, set their own goals, make their own future. That, they said, is the

American way. And that is the dream they offer —
a possible dream, not a fantasy nor a hopeless illu-
sion — but a dream that is anchored in the reality
of a solid record of corporate growth(...) The
Amway business does not claim to offer anyone
guaranteed success. It cannot offer an automatic
cure for every distributor's financial problems. But
at least, it offers a way for the average person to try
to make things better. It offers a dream — and not
just a dream — but a *possible* dream."

Amway is a first-class example of a company
that achieved success through an excellent product
line. Amway has been the leading company in its
field since 1959. It was the first company to introduce a biodegradable detergent, safe for the environment. Nutrilite Double X is the first food sup-
plement in the world to contain vitamins and
minerals.

Did you know that Amway is the only network marketing company to offer top of the line
products such as water filters, parabolic antennas,
security systems for homes ensuring your family's
safety, air filter systems, a prepaid legal service, a
discount travel network, plus mortgage and insurance services? And more.

North-Americans can even buy a car through
the network system. In the United States, Amway
also offers customers MCI telephone services, Visa
charge card, discounted air travel and frequent
flyer miles.

The Amway product line is one of a kind, fully
backed by its 100 % unconditional guarantee. It enjoys an unsurpassed acceptance level by con-

sumers. It is important to note that the company implemented its international marketing network by introducing their line of consumable products. This method enables a distributor to sell repeatedly to the same customers, which in turn provides him/her with more time to increase his/her network through sponsorship.

A large portion of the company's success is largely due to the company's various, yet distinct facilities. The worldwide head office, located in Ada, Michigan, is 910,000 square meters (10,570,248 square feet) and houses offices, the manufacturing plant, research, distribution and other support facilities. In addition, the company owns and leases another 2,212,363 (23,813,875 square feet) square meters in real estate and buildings.

This does not include other installations such as the Nutrilite farm in California where food supplements are grown without chemical fertilizers or pesticides, nor Amway's luxurious resort in Peter Island in the Caribbean. The list goes on and on.

AMWAY Corporation owns a research and development center worth many millions of dollars where more than 250 of the best scientists work in 28 research and development laboratories to improve the constantly expanding product line.

Also, Amway has been a forerunner in ecological and environmental issues for over 35 years. Product quality has always been one of the company's main concerns.

The support system provided to the distributors from Amway as well as their group leaders,
including audio-visual programs, business seminars, training sessions, leadership week-ends and
rallies is really beneficial to each one of them.

Because a company's success or failure can be
attributed to its management, it is important to me
at this point to mention Rich DeVos and Jay Van
Andel, the founders of the company. They have
co-directed the company from its modest begin-
nings in 1959 to its present international success.
The company's business volume was more than 4.5
billion in the fiscal year l992-93.

Furthermore, they have distinguished themselves as prominent figures on the United States
political scene. Jay Van Andel became President of
the board of the United States Chamber of Com-
merce and Rich DeVos became President of the
National Association of Manufacturers and President of the National Direct Selling Association.

Former President George Bush has appointed
Jay Van Andel as U.S. Commissioner General to
Genoa Expo'92. Amway Corporation has been a
major sponsor of the U.S. Pavilion at the fair in
Genoa, Italy, and the Amway Environmental Foundation is sponsoring an exhibit showcasing Amway's environmental sponsorships. The exhibition
in the U.S. Pavilion depicted the importance of our
waterways and the need for their protection. The
Pavilion theme "Beyond the Horizon" not only
captured the spirit of exploration but was a fitted
theme to build an Amway business. With the
world's attention on new horizons and the import-

ance of water in our lives, 1992 was the perfect opportunity to explore new possibilities to promote a quality product from a world-class company: the Amway water treatment system.

Both Rich DeVos and Jay Van Andel have always been very active in the social field and in the arts.

The Amway Environment Foundation

This avant-garde organization is dedicated to the protection of the environment and the development of international awareness on this issue.

A series of five programs have thus been developed to achieve these goals:

Icewalk is an international expedition to the North Pole. The Icewalk expedition for students was designed to train youths in the art of survival and scientific expeditions.

Global Releaf is a national forest preservation campaign launched in cooperation with the American Forestry Association and the Aspen Global Change Institute in order to inform the public on environmental issues.

Masters of the Arctic is a travelling exhibit of contemporary art created by the Inuits of Alaska, the Northwest Territories, northern Quebec, Greenland and Siberia. These works of art tell the story of the Inuit people who lived in harmony with the environment and its resources throughout the last centuries. In fact, Masters of the Arctic is the only exhibit of its kind to have received the diplomatic support of American, Soviet and Canadian missions at the United Nations.

Also, Amway is associated with N.A.S.A., the U.N. Environment Protection Program, and the Windstar Foundation headed by John Denver.

In 1989, the United Nations presented Amway with its prestigious Environmental Award in recognition for its concern for the welfare of our planet. One of only two corporations to receive such an award.

In 1991, the distributors in United States supported again Easter Seals with a donation of more than $1.7 million.

Amway continues to grow and to surpass its most worthwhile competitors because in fact, it surpasses the competition's claims. The energy, the skills and the personal participation of Amway's management, employees and distributors are the key to its unequaled success.

If the financial experts forecast such a wonderful future for network marketing, imagine what part of the market Amway will have within 5 years with over millions of distributors worldwide.

Overall, working with the principles mentioned all along, no other network marketing organization can equal Amway's reputation for product line, company management, individual and collective success stories.

In fact, Amway is responsible for creating the most millionaires in the world of network marketing over the last 35 years.

Souvenir Album
28 years

MILLIONNAIRES D'AMWAY, LES BLANCHARD NOUS OUVRENT LEUR PORTE ET LEUR FORTUNE

LA FAMILLE BLANCHARD

le journal SAMEDI

NUMERO 17, DIMANCHE 12 FÉVRIER

AMWAY
«ON EN VIT, ON EN DORT, ON EN MANGE!»

PAR THÉRÈSE DUMESNIL

«Couple pour travail à temps partiel à la maison. Appelez 000-0000.» — «Temps partiel, revenu supplémentaire. Gens mariés seulement. Tél...» — «Gé-rance pour couples sérieux, travail à domicile.» Ouvrez un journal, n'impor-te lequel, de la feuille de chou locale au grand quotidien, vous y trouverez pres-que à coup sûr une ou plusieurs petites annonces dans ce style. Si, au bout de la ligne, on vous rudoie parce qu'avant de défiler votre état civil, comme au commissariat de police, vous avez l'insolence d'insister pour savoir à qui vous avez affaire et quelle est la nature de travail de couples à domicile qu'on vous dit très agréable; si l'on vous que ça ne s'explique pas au phone, que vous ne comprendriez ... imbécile! —, qu'il faut exacte-une heure et demie de «présenta-avec diapositives pour tout vous si, en somme, on vous propose ...ez-vous mystère auquel on vous ...era par téléphone, fermez les ... rêve est possible: il y a de ...hances que vous soyez en ...cation avec «le Monde d'Am...

..., la dame au bout du fil ne ...ra pas de force à ce rendez-...estin. Au contraire, elle vous ...me la ligne au nez si elle ...otre impertinence, que vous ...a vocation. Il se trouvera ...tard dans votre entourage, ...ur vous enseigner la voie. ... alors à peu près comme ... que vous avez perdu de ...e lurette vous téléphone-...er avec vous. Après les ...ge, il vous glissera qu'il a ...ire pour vous», refusant ...quoi il s'agit et vous ... venir en parler avec ...el moment précis ...endez à une petite ...cortège de voitures ... votre ami vous fera ... qu'il a réuni d'an-...communs! Il vous ... au sous-sol pour ...us faites partie d'un

...rançoise Blanchard, ... ont atteint l'étape ...Diamants, en 1977. ...voyons ici devant ...pte six chambres ...x salles de bain et ...iscine intérieure. ...ne roulotte et un ...ment en Flor... ...qu...

...HEFS DE FILE
...A COMPAGNIE AMWAY
...UÉBEC

Blanchard, grand manitou de Amway
et du Canada.

AMWAY FÊTE
ses meilleurs vendeurs
au Québec

Quelque 3,000 distributeurs de Amway ont vécu, hier, une Journée de rêve au Palais des Congrès! Tous ensemble, confiants dans l'avenir, ils ont rendu hommage aux meilleurs vendeurs du Québec et, ce faisant, ils se sont encouragés mutuellement à persévérer dans cette organisation d'allure pyramidale.

André Dalcourt

Tour à tour, les meilleurs vendeurs des dernières semaines sont montés sur scène, ont prononcé un petit mot et ont recueilli les applaudissements de leurs confrères.

Un biologiste, pour illustrer combien Amway le changeait de son travail, a déclaré: «Amway me permet de travailler sur le cerveau des gens et non plus dedans.»

Tour à tour, les vendeurs se sont dits confiants également de gravir les principaux échelons de l'organisation. Des échelons, il y en a neuf.

Chaque distributeur peut être classé direct, rubis, perle, émeraude, diamant, double diamant, triple diamant, couronne et couronne-ambassadeur.

Des couronnes-ambassadeurs, il y en a une vingtaine dans toute l'Amérique du Nord. Inutile de dire qu'ils profitent à plein de l'American Way of Life.

Amway a été fondée en 1959 par deux individus du Michigan, Richard Devos et Jay Van Endel. Elle offre 3,000 produits en vente. L'an dernier, son chiffre d'affaires a dépassé le milliard de dollars.

Elle est implantée dans 27 pays d'Amérique du Nord, d'Europe et d'Asie. Aucun pays d'Amérique du Sud. «Les gouvernements de ces pays sont trop socialistes, dit André Blanchard, le grand manitou de l'organisation pour l'est du pays. Ils interdisent notre organisation.»

Ici, au pays, Amway a connu certains ennuis avec le fisc ces derniers temps.

Au terme de démêlés juridiques, elle a versé une amende de $25 millions au gouvernement. Mais cela ne l'a pas dérangée! «Des problèmes avec le gouvernement qui n'en a pas! de poursuivre André Blanchard, avec les gouvernements socialistes qu'on a!»

Bienfaisance

En fin d'après-midi, hier, Françoise Blanchard, l'épouse du grand manitou, a pris le micro pour organiser un tirage au profit de son oeuvre de bienfaisance.

Trois billets pour $10. Objectif, $15000.

Avec l'argent, elle compte organiser des week-ends de plein air et un camp de vacances pour des adolescents de 12 à 18 ans.

«Ces week-ends sont extraordinaires a-t-elle déclaré à la foule. Ils permettent de leur enseigner la pensée positive, la foi en Dieu et l'amour de la vie.»

Son époux, André, a confié en aparté: «Cela permet de sortir les jeunes de leur milieu. Bien souvent, ils commencent à s'adonner à la drogue parce qu'ils n'ont pas à la maison l'exemple de parents agressifs. Leurs parents restent là à regarder la télévision et ne s'en occupent pas.»

Une partie des 3,000 convives réunis par Amway.

3,000 vendeurs réunis au Palais des Congrès

Aux convives d'une même table qui, ensemble, allaient donner $100, Françoise Blanchard a promis une invitation à un cocktail chez elle et un bon repas aux frais de son mari dans un grand restaurant de la métropole.

Prenant la parole derrière elle, André Blanchard a ajouté que l'argent recueilli, au-delà de $15,000, jusqu'à concurrence de $5,000, serait versé aujourd'hui au téléthon des Étoiles.

«Nous allons passer à la télévision à 15h07,

Françoise Blanchard s'occupe de l'oeuvre de bienfaisance.

exactement dans le «primetime», a déclaré le grand manitou, clin d'oeil à l'appui. C'est ça avoir des «connections»!

My wife Françoise, with whom I have been building this business for more than 28 years.

From left to right: (Standing) Nathalie, Sébastien, Martin, André. (Sitting) Marie-Josée, Françoise.

On board the "Sea Goddess II",
a Cunard Line luxury liner.

A reception givin in our honour when we reached the
Crown Direct Distributor level. In company of great
friends, Gaétan and Lise Desmarais (left), André and
Hélène Bélair (right), all Diamond Direct Distributors.

With my wife Françoise and our Amway grand-parents Joe and Helyne Victor.

Jay and Betty Van Andel (left) and Rich and Helen DeVos (right), the founders of Amway.

The Montreal Canadien's Stanley Cup Victory in 1964, when I was employed by Couvrette et Provost (Provigo). Fron left to right: André Blanchard, Pierre Mailhot, Henri Richard, René Provost, Gilles Tremblay, Jean Béliveau and the owner of the restaurant where the reception was held.

This business introduced us to some great and well known people such as Mila Mulroney, the Prime Minister's wife, at the Inuit art exhibit, at the Musée de la Civilisation, in Hull, Québec.

During the same evening, in company of the Honourable Joe Clark and his wife Maureen.

During a Diamond Club in company of Rich DeVos and the President of the United States, Gerald Ford.

A reception given in our honour when we reached the Crown Direct Distributor level in 1980. The distributors from our group presented us with this beautiful 1978 Harley Davidson which placed 8th in a contest in Daytona Beach.

Amway offered us a trip in the company jet to the head offices in London, Ontario and Ada, Michigan, when we reached the Double Diamond Direct Distributor level.

We were welcomed by the Executive Committee and the head office staff of Amway Canada.

At the recognition board, at the Michigan head office.

Martin, 21 years old at that time, developing the Amway business in Brazil with his wife. He lived for two years in Brazil. He now lives in Lyon, France, on a permanent basis.

A two month trip to Europe. In the French Alps with our two sons in 1988.

A gift presented to my wife on Father's Day. What a way to celebrate!!!

My 1959 Rolls Royce Silver Shadow, a collection car reserved for important occasions.

Chapter 4

A dream lifestyle!

"When I was courting my wife, I kept telling her that one day, I would give her the moon. Network marketing has been the ladder which allowed me to do it."

What you are looking for is looking for you

My wife and I joined the network in January 1967. At that time, it was usually called multi-level selling. I was then employed as a supervisor for a wholesale food chain. One day, the wife of one of the clients with whom I was doing business, contacted me. She asked me to listen to a concept with which we could make extra money. She was hesitant to approach me with that idea, but she had been told, at a meeting she attended, to talk about it to absolutely everyone she knew without any exceptions and without prejudging. When I think about it today, it wouldn't have taken much for that opportunity to pass me by. Her audacity has been well rewarded.

She approached me by saying: "Mr. Blanchard, would you like to earn extra money per month, and eventually double your revenues in your spare time?" could hardly believe what I was hearing, so I asked her: "Doing what?" She answered: "I can't tell you because I have no experience but there is a meeting at my sister-in-law's home next Sunday afternoon. All I ask is that you trust me and come to the meeting."

I had no reason not to trust her, but I did ask if I could bring my wife. "Of course" she answered, "it would be even better if you do." Instinctively, I knew this was a serious offer and I knew that I would attend the meeting on the following Sunday.

That day, I left work early because I was too excited to keep working. At that time, I was making $70 a week, and someone was offering me a chance to significantly enhance my income, working part-time! As for my skills, all I could have written on a resumé was grade 7 education, and French was the only language I could speak, read or write.

Françoise, my wife, was working as a secretary for a Superior Court judge in Montreal and spoke little English.

We were both raised in a very modest background. Despite this, we were ambitious and both of us had the taste for the beautiful things life could provide. Françoise sewed all her own clothes, many copied from high fashion designs, and we both held one and sometimes two part-time jobs. Occasionally, even a third one.

A first hurdle

This unexpected invitation from our sponsor-to-be to come and look at a business opportunity, really aroused my curiosity. On a scale of 1 to 10, I would say I was right at the top.

When I got home, I told Françoise all about it. Her reaction was totally opposite to what I had expected. She was convinced that such a proposition had to be something entirely illegal. It was too nice to be true, as she said. She did not approve of the invitation and had no intention of attending the business presentation. I remember her saying, "If you think that I'm going to fall for a scam like that, you're sadly mistaken. You can go if you want to, but don't count on me. It's out of the question. Forget it."

As for myself, I kept on dreaming and wondering what this intriguing invitation was all about. Regardless of what my wife thought, I fully intended to keep my appointment for that coming Sunday because I had complete faith in the people who had invited me.

On the appointed day, I managed to convince Françoise to accompany me. The long drive there was done in silence. The only reason she came was to protect me. Her reaction was even stronger when we reached the meeting place and she saw a black Cadillac with New York licence plates, parked in front of the house where we were going. We both had the feeling that we had been taken in and were going to be the victims of con artists. I had to convince her to go in. She really panicked when we entered. Someone was directing men and women to separate rooms in the house. The worry subsided when we realized it was only to put away our winter coats.

The presentation was done in a combination of French and English by Monique Laforce, a Franco-American from Syracuse, New York. She was bubbly and enthusiastic and she convinced me that opportunity was indeed knocking at our door.

I was so wound up, I could hardly contain myself. I knew this was a serious business. Françoise, on the other hand, felt ill at ease. She was not paying attention, and in fact was impatient to get out of there.

At the end of the meeting, they attempted to make us join the network but Françoise was too skeptical. She asked for a copy of the application form so that her boss, the honourable judge, could scrutinize it.

A second hurdle

On our way home, I thought I had managed to transfer my enthusiasm to my wife, but she lost it the moment we got home. When I started to explain the plan to our baby-sitter, my mother-in-law, she immediately advised us not to consider such a trivial project, adding that it would never work in Quebec. This unsolicited advice was all it took for Françoise to completely lose all interest in the idea. However, it only served to strengthen my own resolve as I told myself: SUCCESS IS THE BEST

REVENGE! I *can* and I *will* succeed, just to prove them wrong.

That same evening, on a piece of paper, I began to draw circles, similar to those at the presentation. I calculated and estimated what the income could be if one was to commit himself completely to the plan and sponsor approximately fifty persons who would generate a sales volume of approximately $500 a month each. After paying the distributors' bonuses, I would have a tidy profit left. Wow!

After drafting the plan on paper, I showed it to Françoise who said: "You have lost your mind. You're daydreaming. Come back down to earth. You know that it is not possible. Stop dreaming and do something more productive."

In spite of all her sarcasm and efforts to change my mind, she could not shake my confidence. I was already mentally and emotionally "committed" to see this through.

It is not the day you join that is important, it is the moment that it gets into your blood. My two jokers did the job!

All these figures were so stimulating that instead of throwing out my projections, I pinned the paper to the inside of my jewelry box. Every day, morning and night, I saw my dream, filed it away in my subconscious and anchored my will to succeed. I did not know at the time that I was using one of the best methods there is to reach one's goals.

With all these great plans rambling through my mind, I told myself that if I only managed to earn an extra $60.00 a month with this business, I could quit my part-time job of selling shoes on weekends. This would give me more time to spend with my family. Françoise and I had one child at the time and she was six month pregnant of a second daughter.

I decided to attend a second meeting which was held a month later, on January 20, 1967. Françoise came along because she was told that only the person(s) registered on the registration form could attend the all-expense paid Amway Direct Distributors seminar. She was afraid that I would go alone. She was reluctant to sell and contact people and did not really want to participate.

A simple start

At first, I began developing my business only during my spare time.

I worked alone during the first three months because Françoise had decided not to get involved. Still working part-time in a shoe store every weekend, I did not have much time to invest. The only free time I did have was Wednesday evenings and Sunday afternoons. However, the one thing that I had plenty of was my burning desire to succeed.

From the first meeting I attended, I remembered that Monique Laforce spoke about the 45 year plan versus a 2 to 5 year plan. I had already decided and chosen to work very hard for myself for two to five years, rather than work for someone else for 45 years and end up with a small retirement pension and a watch.

Even after joining this organization, I had no idea what I had to do next, so I asked Monique Laforce how to get a good start in the business. She told me to organize a meeting in my home, and show the marketing plan to people I knew. She said that she would not be returning to this area for another month and that I would have to manage by myself, with the help of my sponsor. Convinced that her recipe was the true answer to build this business, I decided to invite everybody that I could think of to my first meeting. That included all my aunts and uncles and various friends.

My sponsor, only a week old in the business himself, but somewhat a little more experienced than I was, helped me out. His presentation lasted all of ten minutes. That was all he knew. My input that day was showing everyone some of the commonly used products which were available at the time. That lasted all of another ten minutes.

Impressive, don't you think? Not as far as I was concerned, because my forty guests had a cup of coffee and a donut, and left without joining. Not even one. The last one that left said: "André, you'll be good in this!"

That is when Françoise told me: "You see, now we are forty-one against you. You will have to manage without me." That was all I needed to urge me on and I replied: "I know people who are more intelligent and more ambitious, and I will find them!"

I then decided to commit myself even more and to rely on no one but myself. I prepared the meeting by writing down my presentation on a large piece of cardboard. I had no other material, no experience, and had not involved my sponsor (just in case he failed once again). I just could not take that risk. I organized my first solo meeting. I was expecting fifteen people, but only four showed up. But miracle of miracles! Two men who came as "scouts", without their wives, decided to join.

Ironically, a great part of our organization today comes from those two initial distributorships. What if I would have quit after my first meeting?

Three months later

During the first month, I managed to sponsor seven distributors. During the second month, I added eight more. They all quit almost as soon as they got in. They helped me realize that people who have no dreams or goals will complain about the noise opportunity makes when it knocks at their door.

My determination to succeed kept me going. I continued striving to get ahead. Finally, after three months in the business, Françoise recognized the potential that this opportunity presented. She also realized that I would succeed, with or without her.

I had managed to turn her around. First, by sheer determination, but then in a more subtle way. I showed her my monthly result and bought her a patio set, paid for entirely with the profits from my business. That was the day she really became my business partner.

I knew that with her help, we could work as a team to accomplish our goals, and that we would achieve them faster and go further working together. We have always been hard workers and were willing to help others. Zig Ziglar, author of *See You at the Top* says: "You can get all you want from life if you help others get what they want." My business life is based on that very principle.

A smashing success

Only one month after deciding to help me build the business, Françoise gave birth to our second daughter. The following month, in June 1967, we reached the much coveted level of Direct Distributor. By doing so, we were now being paid at the highest percentage on the performance-bonus scale.

Our personal experience made us attain this level after only being in the business for five months. I had doubled my income in spite of the sizeable obstacles we had to face, as well as the fact that all the product labels and information were in English only. At that time, we were conducting our business in an entirely French environment. In addition, not only did we have just one line of household products, but we were also having many supply problems mostly encountered by new and growing businesses.

In August of that same year, I asked my boss for one week vacation without pay to attend our

Direct Distributor seminar in Michigan, all expenses paid by the company. He refused. The realization that I was enslaved by the system, and that I was getting nowhere, really opened my eyes. I handed in my resignation in order to work full-time at building our business. When I told Françoise what I had done, she literally panicked. She believed firmly in the so called security of a job and could not see how the business would allow us to make ends meet.

This situation caused endless frustations. Money was the one subject we mostly talked about, but could never agree on, as was and still is the case for too many couples. I had already resigned and Françoise felt trapped. Since these events occurred during her vacation, she reassured herself by thinking that at least her salary would be our lifesaver.

She soon realized however, that although most people were still running out of money long before the end of the month, we always had money left over in our wallets after having paid all our monthly bills.

Two months later, things were going so well and moving at such a rapid pace that she also resigned. Her optimism had overcome her fears and her doubts. She never regretted her decision, knowing that we could never have achieved so much, in so little time, if we had kept working at full and part time jobs.

We continued achieving success after success, and after only sixteen months of effort, we reached a much coveted level of leadership in the Amway organization. We had qualified as Diamond Direct Distributors.

The company reacted quickly to our rapid growth, and its expansion in the Province of Quebec, the french part of Canada. All of our product labels and literature were translated into French.

Eventually, we qualified for all available trips, including many to Hawaii, as well as Hong Kong, Switzerland, Thailand, Brazil, and two cruises on the Sea Goddess, a luxury cruise ship of the Cunard Line. Many other cruises were enjoyed on the Enterprise, Amway's well known private yacht. The cruises took us to Peter Island, Amway's property in the Caribbean, as well as to many other destinations. We had travelled the world before we reached the age of 40.

To summarize, five months after joining, we reached Direct Distributor level in June 1967. That same year, we attained the Ruby and Pearl levels. We reached Emerald and Diamond in 1968, barely sixteen months after joining. We reached Double Diamond in 1973, Triple Diamond in 1977, and became Crown Directs in March 1980. We know however that we climbed the steps to success rapidly but we are well aware that it is not necessarely the same for everyone. One thing is sure, we believed in our dreams.

A resounding success

From the very beginning, we qualified for all the trips Amway offered, along with the seminars on leadership and those intended for Direct Distributors, Diamonds, and Executive Diamonds.

The growth of our business is one of the most rapid in Amway's history and has remained unequalled after 25 years.

Beyond all expectations

From the very beginning of our association with Amway, I could visualize myself boarding a plane for France and explaining the marketing plan to French people. The company representatives had always said that maybe one day Amway would expand to other countries. I wanted it to be France because as you know, French was the only language I was fluent in at the time. Since that time, many countries have opened their doors to the wonderful world of Amway.

When Amway decides to penetrate a new market, it takes care of all the legal steps to set up offices and operate a distribution center. Then the company representatives announce the opening to the distributors. It is up to the distributors to decide if they want to invest time and money to develop that market share.

In fact, this is exactly what happened in 1977. France welcomed Amway with open arms, giving distributors from other countries the chance to meet their contacts for potential sponsoring. We were involved in this new venture from the very beginning with a group of distributors from Quebec. I arrived in France with a long list of referrals given to me by distributors from Quebec. I met with them individually or in groups. It was an instant success because France was able to adjust to a system that gave an opportunity to people wishing to change their lifestyle. They had all the proofs they needed. Hundreds of couples in the United States and Canada had a tremendous success with network marketing, and there was no reason why individuals in other countries could not do the same.

Eventually, our organization grew internationally. At first, it happened in a manner typical of network marketing where each person within the network called upon his/her personal contacts (family and friends) for business purposes. Then, in a more systematic manner, we decided to invest energy, time and money. I believed in the potential and that prompted me to improve my English, to learn Spanish, Italian and Portugese and subsequently to take part in the development of the Amway organization throughout Europe.

Our involvement was such that 28 years later, we are doing business in over 15 countries throughout the world and we are personally active not only in Canada, but also in France, Spain, Italy, Portugal, Germany, Poland, Argentina, Hungary, Brazil, Mexico and the United States. Greece and China will follow when Amway opens up there in the very near future.

As a result, we have established deep relationships and have made many friends all over the world while building this business on the international scene. We get to meet with them often on the various seminars and trips that Amway provides for us all.

The world holds no secrets for me. I know all the ways to facilitate travelling. I have developped a fondness and desire for studying other nations and their languages. Putting together a complex itinerary is as easy for me as cooking ham and eggs.

What still fascinates and pleases both Françoise and myself is to be welcomed into people's homes and invited to share a drink or a meal with the individuals we meet in the various countries we visit. Instead of only visiting churches and museums like tourists do, we get also to know people, discover and share cultural differences which is so much more enriching.

Economic repercussions

We have met thousands of people throughout the years and although it is difficult to keep track of all the people who are involved with our organization (it is somewhat like tracing a family tree), we estimate that our organization is made up of approximately 100,000 people. The beauty of it is that it just keeps on growing.

An active participation

Subsequently, our many years experience and our active participation with Amway has enabled both my wife and myself to be elected to the Board of Directors of the Amway Distributors Association of Canada. I have personally been involved with the Board for 15 years as a Director and also as President. Françoise has been President of the Board ending her term in 1993.

A philosophy of life

It is very important to us that all aspects of our life that is, family, social, spiritual, physical, professional and financial become totally fulfilled. Besides, with Françoise being a perfectionist, it could hardly be otherwise. She believes that she would never agree to trade in any of her basic human values simply for financial gain.

Earning money, more money, and even more money than one can expect without trying to find a sense of balance in one's life, can sometimes create chaos. This is undoubtedly what has lead people to say: "Money does not buy happiness." Besides, when one searches for a balance in life, there is no doubt that money becomes a blessing from heaven.

Money provided us with the security to comfortably raise our four children. It was also beneficial to us because we no longer argued about it. It had eliminated the frequent frustrations many couples experience in daily life (the same ones we were facing not long before). Consequently, we were able to develop an excellent line of communication between us.

As Françoise likes to say, communication is the key to understanding. In order to really understand one another, we have to share thoughts and not just talk about meaningless daily events, but serious dialogue about how we feel, and where we are heading together. If we are going to work as a team in life, as well as in business, neither one of us can hide in a glass bubble.

This special friendship, based on mutual collaboration, is responsible for the success of our marriage which in turn, had a positive effect on the success of our business.

Growing in the business world

During our countless trips to the United States, we quickly became aware that many Americans had developped a distinct positive mental attitude. We also noticed that there was an abundance of reading material available, thanks to the large number of well-known authors and speakers specializing in this field.

At that stage in my life, I had managed to learn english well enough to take advantage of these great books, but unfortunately the vast majority of our French distributors could not.

I promptly asked a publisher to translate and publish one of these books. Unfortunately, the publisher I contacted wanted me to invest a large sum of money and guarantee him a large order, all paid in advance.

When I told Françoise that I wanted to start a publishing business, she doubted I could accomplish this with only a grade seven education. That was all I needed to make a decision to start my publishing business dealing with books on self-improvement and positive thinking. As soon as the idea crossed my mind, I set it into motion. Jokingly, I said, "Why not call it A Different World Publishing Company?" (In French: Les éditions Un monde différent ltée)

That is how the publishing company was launched in 1977, at a time when very few people in Quebec believed in this market potential.

We mostly publish books on self-improvement. These have helped us improve the way we think, act and react, which in turn has a positive effect on our family. This change is even more apparent with my wife. She has undergone great changes in her quest for self-fulfillment. Formerly a suspicious person with a negative attitude and always ready to criticize, she became an assertive, strong and positive thinking individual. Her motto is: "There isn't anything or anyone strong enough to keep me from being the person I want to be, or to stop me from getting everything I deserve and want out of life".

Today, "Les éditions Un monde différent ltée", a world leader in the production of French books and tapes on motivation and self-help, has proven its worth in helping individuals who wish to move ahead.

One of my friends, a successful Montreal lawyer, gave me this moving testimony when he said: "You will never know how much you have helped french readers grow with your publishing company."

The fact remains, that these books have helped us move forward, and at the same time helped thousands of others. What a satisfying achievement it is to be unable to measure the amount of good we may have generated around us.

From generation to generation

Like all parents, we are truly proud and happy that our four children, now adults, have chosen to follow in our footsteps. Whether they work for our publishing company, or as individual Amway distributors, we know that they have that desire to succeed, and that gives me great satisfaction.

Marie-Josée, our oldest, born on Christmas day 1964, is building her Amway business. She has reached the Ruby Direct Distributor level and has great plans for her future. She plans on expanding her business worldwide and visiting her distributors in many countries. As publisher of our monthly newsletter, Marie-Josée is also in close contact with the distributors of our organization.

Nathalie, a very dynamic young woman, is the editor of our publishing company. An artist at heart, she invests all her energy in her career. She loves the creative aspect of her work and is most happy when she can put her natural talents to good use. She is also a distributor and heads a large organization in Italy.

As for Martin, born in 1970, when he turned 18, he decided to pursue a career as a sound engineer. He attended a private school in Montreal to earn his degree and for a few years made a career of working at our large meetings as sound man. He would provide us with music, tape all our meetings, then duplicate these as instructional and motivational tapes, basic tools in this business. Since his birth, Martin, a product of his environment, has always been involved with the distributors in our business and the spirit that makes it move ahead. He soon decided to start his own career with Amway. He has chosen to follow in our footsteps on the international scene. He spent four months in Europe in the summer of 1991, meeting and sponsoring distributors while building his business. He lived in Sao Paulo, Brazil for two years, and developped one of the largest network in the world of Amway. He now lives in Lyon, France, where he is currently developing his network.

When Martin left for Europe, he handed down his recording company to his younger brother Sébastien, then old enough to be fully involved in the family business. No one can predict his future but his dream is to become a Crown Ambassador in Amway. We hope his dream will come true. Sebastien has decided to pursuit a new career in going back to school, working his network at the same time.

We gave our children the freedom to chose their own careers. They have lived their whole life with parents involved in building a large scale business that very often offered extraordinary rewards. Our children learned, through contacts with wonderful people, that life has marvelous possibilities, and that they can be a part of it all. In other words, they shared in our lifestyle and in doing so, learned that they also have potential and are entitled to the best that life has to offer. Besides, without a positive self-image, it is impossible to perform in any field.

Leisure

Physical well-being has always been an important factor in our lives.

I find golf to be the best form of physical relaxation. I even invested in a golf course to keep in touch with the sport. One of my fondest memories is having played golf in Hawaii at a course built on volcanic rock. What beautiful scenery!

I read everything I can get my hands on, which is the reason why I can get involved in conversations on many topics. You have also probably concluded by now that I love to travel and to learn about the customs of people in the countries where I travel. I really appreciate the fact that I can coordinate many meetings but still find the time to maintain a good physical regime in order to stay in shape.

Françoise, on the other hand, prefers and enjoys reading over any other activity. She will occasionally go downhill skiing and the Rockies are her favorite mountains. She loves to be a speaker in small or large groups. The microphone brings out her many talents as a speaker. She loves to increase people's awareness of the potential a free enterprise business like Amway has to offer. Above all else she searches for serenity and balance in life. She loves to live life with enthusiasm and excitement.

Our lakefront home is a quiet place where we can relax, and we use that time to meditate and bring ourselves to peak mental fitness.

We firmly believe that we are the product of our environment. "Tell me who your friends are, and I will tell you who you are." To this we add, "Tell me what you read and I will tell you what you will become."

Aim high

Very few people remain enthusiastic about their career after 28 years. In our case, we are more excited about it than we have ever been. Everyone spends so much time creating something worthwhile and lasting through a career, that I cannot imagine being enslaved to a job for a lifetime. I could never have accepted that.

Each career or profession offers not only benefits but also challenges and one feels a deep sense of satisfaction in conquering each and everyone of those challenges.

Dreams and more dreams!

Dreams come in all shapes and sizes. Have all *my* dreams come true? The answer is no, however, those that became reality did not always come true exactly at the prescribed time. Nevertheless, it is much more rewarding to focus on results and rewards than on efforts. Should we let go of dreams that don't come true when we want them to? Never. We have to adjust, reschedule and go on because we are always much closer to reaching that goal than we believe. It is always too soon to throw in the towel.

Smell the roses

Rewarding ourselves is a very important aspect in remaining motivated, and maintaining our desire to work or to build a business. We must take the time to smell the roses along the way.

You will surely agree with me that it is much more enjoyable to shop for things that you like, rather than constantly look at the price tags. Furthermore, it is always much more pleasant to select meals from the left column of the menu rather than the right one whenever you are in a nice restaurant.

Beyond the tangible

Despite all the obvious benefits that the material rewards provide, the skills and the talents which we develop are what really shape our personalities. Among the basic qualities which help people become successful, I would list self-confidence, the desire to succeed, the unequivocal decision to do whatever it takes, charisma, dedication and ambition.

Futhermore, there are certain areas in our lives which must follow order such as priorities, dreams, goals, an action plan and preferably in that order. Most people resist change and, unfortunately, in refusing to modify the way we think and act, we allow a rich and satisfying life to pass us by.

Remember, fear is a negative feeling that hinders growth and hope is the positive aspect that helps success to flourish.

Our values

Without a doubt, our three greatest assets are good health, the proper use of time and the freedom of choice.

Without good health, it is impossible to generate the maximum effort required to reach our objectives. Françoise and I have developed better health habits such as eating more fruits and vegetables, cutting down on certain meats, drinking in moderation and most importantly, we do not smoke. I have always said that I could never have stayed in such good shape, nor worked as many long hours, nor travelled throughout the world eating all types of food at all hours, nor coped with the jet lag had it not been for the food supplements I take every day.

Time is a commodity that we all equally share. It is what I call "the fair side of life". Choosing what we do with that time is an art that will determine our level of success in life. Naturally, if an individual chooses to spend all his time playing, drinking or doing other meaningless activities, that individual should not be surprised by the lack of accomplishment in his life.

Freedom of choice is our greatest power: we choose how we think, how we act, how we work, study, even how we select our friends, our spouse, etc. In retrospect, we sometimes realize that if we did not always make the best choice it can simply be rectified by making new choices. At any rate, I have tried to learn a lesson from all the "bad" choices I made in the past. Life is a school with lessons and homework and learning will always be the best way for us to grow, for as long as we live.

It is imperative that we make our choices carefully because they have a major influence on the direction we take. For example, if Françoise and I had decided not to build our Amway business or if we had decided to quit along the way, where would we be today? The thought of it gives me goose bumps.

Life is a bank account

Life is a bank account. Too many people want to make withdrawals before they have made a deposit. As a young boy scout, I learned that giving for the love of giving is one of life's greatest satisfactions. It is incredible how generosity really attracts generosity. I firmly believe that life is governed by the boomerang principle. Everything we give is given back to us in abundance, but everything we choose to hold back is taken back, also in abundance.

A balance in life

To my way of thinking, our most significant achievements are based on a delicate balance in matters of the head and of the heart. Some people are emotionally attracted to certain ideas but do not think logically about the consequences; whereas others are so rational that they analyze everything without ever involving their emotions, their heart.

Then, there are those who get carried away and give up everything to go with the flow, sometimes to the right and other times to the left. It is important to follow a certain rhythm because, like dancing, you may step on someonelse's toes.

A second nature

Someone once asked me how many hours a day I spend in my business. I replied "24 hours a day". He seemed surprised. I added that I thought about success 24 hours a day and as a result, my business had become second nature to me, a way of life and maybe a sixth sense.

If I speak to someone for more than ten minutes, the topic of conversation will inevitably shift to network marketing.

A common problem among the majority of people is that very few ever plan for their old age. I once received a brochure which showed what will happen to 100 people, all 25 years of age. Sixty-four of them will reach the age of 65 and thirty-six will be dead before that age. Of the 64 persons, 4 will be financially independent, only one will be rich, 5 will still be working and 54 will be dependent on others. I asked myself; if only 1 out of 100 is to become rich, why shouldn't it be me? The study also mentioned that most people are poorer at 65 than they were at 25, after 40 to 45 years of hard work.

I have never wanted nor accepted becoming part of the negative side of those statistics. I have always been convinced that I was born to succeed. I have invested all my energy into this ideal business. I was convinced I would succeed. I had a date with fate.

During the past 28 years, I have never once doubted that happiness and success would always be there for me.

WHEN YOU HAVE A PROBLEM:

DO SOMETHING ABOUT IT!

IF YOU CANNOT GO OVER IT:
GO UNDER IT, GO THROUGH IT,
GO AROUND IT, GO TO THE RIGHT,
GO TO THE LEFT.

IF THE RIGHT MATERIAL IS UNAVAILABLE:
GO FIND IT;

IF YOU CANNOT FIND IT: REPLACE IT;

IF YOU CANNOT REPLACE IT; IMPROVISE;

IF YOU CANNOT IMPROVISE: INNOVATE.

BUT THE MOST IMPORTANT THING IS TO DO
SOMETHING ABOUT IT! THERE ARE TWO
KINDS OF PEOPLE WHO NEVER AMOUNT TO
MUCH:
THOSE WHO DO NOT WANT TO DO
ANYTHING AND THOSE WHO FIND EXCUSES.

"Success is the best revenge"

Chapter 5

Be convinced and you will be convincing

Convince through emotions

It all begins when someone introduces you to network marketing, either on a white board or on a sheet of paper. But once you have seen it the notion will haunt your mind forever. Personally, I was so excited by network marketing that I saw circles everywhere. They filled my mind. Once you have seen them, your first step is to take a sheet of paper and draw out your plan of action, and your list of contacts. The next step of the process is simply to put the plan into action; make it concrete.

Always remember that most people make most decisions based on emotion, not logic. If people believe what you say, they will do anything to succeed.

Therefore, it is important to learn to talk to people. When you introduce your program, make it touch them personally and make your presentation one that appeals to their emotions.

The last laugh!

There has never been a better time to get things done than right now, whether for yourself or for your prospects. You can rest assured that circumstances will *never* be ideal. You have to learn to make things happen. Ask yourself this: "Do I wait for perfect weather, and until all the traffic lights are green before I go to work every morning?"

Of course not. You simply leave the house and adapt as you go. So do not sit around waiting for the perfect time. Do it *now*!

In a business like this one, there is no office to rent or equipment to install in order to get started. The only major base that you want to cover is rather unique. It simply consists of preparing yourself mentally, of building an unwavering positive mental attitude that will overcome all adverse circumstances that might come your way. Focus on your dreams.

All your present friends, acquaintances, relatives and family will not necessarily be on your positive mental wave length. You will have to put up with their refusals, their laughters, and even with sarcastic remarks from people you thought were your best friends.

I always tell the new people in our organization that one of the first things they should do is find themselves a "joker". That is someone who will laugh at your ideas and your plans for success. They will fortify your personal convictions to want success even more than you do now.

If you cannot find anyone who disagrees with you, give me a call. I still know some skeptics that I can send your way.

Sweet revenge

There will always be those who say: "We are not interested, but *you* will no doubt succeed in this business."

This happened to me at that first meeting where I had invited my friends and family — everyone I thought I knew at the time. All forty of them said NO.

If this ever happens to you and you are the least bit ambitious, as I was, you will want to prove these people wrong by simply going out and succeeding without them.

I never wanted to be in a situation where a friend or a member of my family could one day say to me: "I knew you would not succeed!"

It is then that I decided that my success would be my way of revenge against those who helped me to succeed by making fun of me and laughing at my dreams. More importantly, it was a revenge against my past, my shyness and more specifically, my lack of education.

The best way to develop a strong positive mental attitude that will last, is to surround yourself with successful people. Curiously, successful people never try to discourage someone who wishes to undertake a new venture. Quite the opposite, they usually encourage new experiences.

Tell me who your friends are

We have all heard: "Tell me who your friends are, and I will tell you who you are." So, if you are not in daily contact with successful people, if you do not read books or listen to tapes about achieving success, or if you do not attend meetings organized by your leaders, you are shutting the door on all of your resources, especially your success.

Even if you have the best of attitudes, you must first and foremost, be convinced of the benefits of network marketing if you want to gain support for your cause.

Be convinced of the benefits of network marketing

Let's return to the ideal business we spoke of earlier, and review its main characteristics:

In network marketing:

You are in business for yourself.

You are the boss.

You make up your own schedule.

Your territory has no boundaries.

You sponsor where you want and live where you want.

You do not need employees.

You choose the people with whom you want to build your business.

You do not need to invest any money for luxurious office space.

You have tax benefits.

There are no accounts receivable.

You develop your own leadership and personal skills.

You build your own business, one that you can pass on to your legal heirs.

You distribute quality products and services.

Proof at Hand

Insofar as my Amway distributorship is concerned, I love the fact that the products I distribute are all top quality, as well as concentrated and environmentally friendly.

With an Amway distributorship, there is always the possibility to expand internationally. In fact, at the present time, it is possible to sponsor in 60 countries and territories. This decade will see Amway expanding even more into Eastern Europe, South America and the Pacific Rim. The globalization of markets that we have been hearing about for the last few years has long been a way of life at Amway.

As for the stability of this business, you cannot ask for anything better. In our 28 years in the business, we have met people who, for personal reasons, had to reduce the efforts they would normally put into their networking business. Their business just kept on generating monthly income.

If you are presently working and paid on a commission basis, how long will the company continue to pay you if you leave for a certain period of time?

Always be on guard for companies who do not always have the necessary funds to continue paying you, for sooner or later, that same lack of funds will cause them to disappear.

In the Amway business, the founders have always reinvested their money in order to face any unexpected eventuality.

A living proof

I mentioned earlier that I only had a grade seven education, little money, but a great deal of ambition when I joined the business.

However, I realized that in order to expand my business and increase my sales volume, I needed to simplify product pick-up for my distributors. So, I decided to borrow the money I needed to increase my inventory. The bank manager, however did not share my optimism towards my business. He did not want to lend me the money that I needed. So I simply readjusted my strategy and requested a loan to renovate my basement. It was close enough to the truth because I covered the walls with products.

It is possible that my bank manager then still does not believe in my business even though he lost his job three years later. He actually thought that his job provided him with better security than my business! On the other hand, I realized from the start the potential this business had to offer. I firmly believed in it. That is probably what is called a visionary attitude.

A winning attitude

1. A winner says: "Let's find the answer"; a loser says: "Nobody knows that."

2. A winner who makes a mistake says: "I made a mistake"; a loser who makes a mistake says: "It's not my fault."

3. A winner overcomes a problem; a loser digs his own grave and never manages to get out of it.

4. A winner commits; a loser makes promises.

5. A winner says: "I am good but I can improve myself." A loser says: "I am no worse than many others."

6. A winner tries to learn from those who are better than himself; a loser tries to tear down those who are better than himself.

7. A winner says: "There has to be a better way to succeed"; a loser says: "That's the way it has always been done".

Part Three:

The Success System

> *"Work is love made visible".*
>
> Kahlil Gibran

Chapter 6

How to Build an Organization

In your opinion, what are the most important things in life, after health and love? My answer would have to be contacts, human contacts, sharing, exchanging, negotiating, and dialogue. It is very important to have relationships with others, for this is really the true driving force of network marketing.

The first step in network marketing is to sponsor someone. Your upline will help you in sponsoring your first distributors. Beginners regard this type of support with awe. It is not something they expect in a conventional business. This type of help also encourages and motivates beginners to build an organization right from the start.

Another interesting factor to keep in mind is the operational structure of the group you are joining, as well as the support system and training that is provided for you. It can make a big difference and will greatly improve your chances for success.

A) The importance of the success system

Your main responsibility as a member of a marketing network is to offer encouragement to each person in your network and teach them the pattern of success. However, each party must be willing to do his/her share. Network marketing is a program which helps people who are willing to help themselves.

I have learned one important thing, and that is not to try to reinvent the wheel. There are excellent methods to achieve success and these have all been well tested. All you have to do is apply them and follow them to the letter.

The secret of success is to repeat time after time, using only methods and ideas that work, no matter how insignificant they may seem. Let's compare this repetition process to how mother nature builds huge, often gigantic stalagmites found in caves around the world.

Continuous drops of calcium filled water keep dripping from the roof of the cave, drop, after drop, after drop. Over time these tiny deposits of calcium form a huge solid foundation for a column that eventually grows big and high enough to unite with the stalagmites above.

Similarly, you will come to realize that by constantly repeating actions that are proven to be effective, you'll eventually reach your peak in the business as well.

How to help someone to develop his network

1. *Assess your associate*

It is important that you get to know your new distributor well from the start. Find out what kind of an individual he is, and get a handle on what could motivate him to bigger and better things. Eventually, you will be in a position to decide if he is worth the time you plan to invest with him.

To help you evaluate your distributor, ask these five questions:

1) If I show you a method to help build your financial independence and gain security, would you be interested?

2) Are you ready to invest 10 to 15 hours a week to help make this plan work for you?

3) Can you attend at least one meeting a week?

4) Are you ready to make up a list of all the people you know, without prejudging any of them?

5) Would you invite some of them to a meeting that I would hold in your home next Tuesday at 8 p.m.?

If your associate answers yes to all of these questions, you are talking to someone who is motivated and interested.

If he answers no to any of these questions, do not insist. Help him sponsor other people in order to find someone in his group who will answer yes to all five questions. Do not hesitate to invest your time to help that individual. Working in depth is a key to grow in this business.

Profile of leaders

Not all the people who join your network will be worthy of your attention. If they are not serious, do not waste your time motivating them to be what they do not wish to be.

One of the most common mistakes is that oftentimes, someone will sponsor a dynamic distributor and then lets that person build by him/herself, because he/she does not seem to need any help. Instead of helping this person by investing profitable time, they waste their time helping someone who claims to be interested, but who is in fact unwilling to make the necessary efforts. Your time *must* be invested with serious and ambitious people.

You will recognize future leaders by their willingness to learn more through meetings, tapes and books on motivation and techniques that you recommend to them. Another way that you'll recognize them easily is that future leaders have a positive mental attitude, a tremendous ability to draw up an impressive list of people and they are willing to eagerly call every person on the list. They regularly call you for all kinds of information and to tell you about the marvellous things that are happening to them or in their group. These are the people you want to work with, and once they have built a strong group, one that grows regularly in width and in depth, without your ongoing involvement, you can then take the time to develop other personal groups.

The 20/80 law

Keep in mind Pareto's Law, the one that states that 20 % of your group will produce 80 % of the results, and that 80 % of your group will only produce 20 % of the results. Which ones that should benefit from 80 % of your time?

Therefore, learn to assess your associates and invest your time wisely with the appropriate people. It is very important at this stage to know what you are going to teach them. If in doubt, consult upline.

2.   *Teach them the ABC'S of the perfect distributor*

The basic steps of network marketing that you should teach your new associates are as follows:

First, help them draw a list of at least 50 names of people they know. Help them recall their neighbours, their family members, their children's friends, the people on their Christmas card list, the guests at their wedding, their colleagues, their sport partners, church members, etc.

Second, teach them what to say when they invite their friends to the business presentations. Ideally, you should be there when they make the first calls. Then, book a meeting for them, and also let them know where the next group meeting will be. Remind them that their first meeting can be held around the kitchen table and it can be with just a few people. You want them to experience success quickly in order to encourage them to keep on going. Try to make it as easy as you can for them. Then you will see how that first success, no matter how small it is, can make a world of difference for them.

Third, I recommend that you keep a close watch over a new distributor until he has at least five or six good distributors in each of three of his groups. Make sure that some of them are duplicating what you are doing. This is *very* important, because if no one is duplicating you, you can wind up with people doing nothing. Even though you have in your group a large number of distributors, no financial gain will be generated without merchandising the products.

B) Merchandising

The marketing aspect of network marketing is divided into two main areas which require our ongoing efforts: *distribution* of products and services, and *sponsoring*. Sponsoring is that aspect of the business where you sponsor someone, who in turn sponsors someone else, and so on. This is the true principle of duplication. Ex.: if you only personally sponsor 2 a month for 10 months.

$$2 + 2 + 2 + 2 + 2 + 2 + 2 + 2 + 2 + 2 = \ 20$$

But: if you sponsor l a month who sponsors l a month, and so on for 10 months, look at the results now.

$$2 \times 2 \times 2 \times 2 \times 2 \times 2 \times 2 \times 2 \times 2 \times 2 = 1\ 024$$

1. *Distribution*

a. Use your products

First, be familiar with your products. The only way that you can gain first-hand experience about the quality of your products and services, and know how effective they really are, is to use them yourself. There is no other way. Remember — you now build your own business. Why would you want to support the competition by buying and using their products? Get your new distributors to do the same thing.

The impact of doing it can generate an increase of several thousands of dollars for your business. How could you convince someone that Amway products are better if you use brand X? This could cost you a potential distributor and some very good customers. Every second you hesitate converting over to your own products and services is costing you money. Take brand X products that you still have in your home and give them to those people who did not take you seriously. If nothing else, they will certainly be intrigued and wonder what the heck you are up to in this mysterious business of yours.

b.   **Retail and wholesale distribution**

Let's talk about the retail distribution of your products to Mr. and Mrs. Consumer.

Many people strongly dislike the word "sales" and the whole idea of selling. Yet, everybody sells every day... "Susan, did you see the new movie? It's really great!" "Harry, try my dessert, it's delicious!" "Honey, let's get married!" That is probably the best sale you *ever* made.

If the idea of using the word "sell" bothers you, simply change the terminology to: provide, serve, supply, merchandise or satisfy a need. One of the biggest fears a beginner may face in this business is actually selling products to someone.

At times, it may be harder to sell to friends than to strangers. That is why it is so important to know that you are associated with a reliable, well established company whose credibility and product quality is well known and appreciated by consumers and distributors alike. This makes it much easier for beginners and it reassures them that they are investing their time wisely.

To illustrate the point, let me tell you about Françoise when she was first introduced to the business. She indicated clearly that there were two things she simply refused to do: sell products and speak to people!!! At the time she was a secretary for a Judge in Superior Court, in Montreal. She would tell her co-workers how much she liked the new products she was using. She told them she was buying them from a *friend*. She must have been convincing, because the other secretaries said they would like to try these products also. Françoise told them she would speak to her friend and get them what they needed. She was still too shy to admit that we were the ones selling the products. However, they soon found out that we were operating our own business, because Françoise simply could not suppress her enthusiasm any longer.

In any event, do not let the distribution or retail side of the business scare you. In a regular retail business, retail sales counts for 100 % of the business. In network marketing, however, retail sales account for a very small portion of your business. Some distributors give their regular customers a bonus when they either purchase a certain product or refer them to another customer. This is a great way to motivate someone to become a steady customer if they originally were not interested in becoming a distributor.

A doctor in our group recently told me just how much this business motivated him. He had just sold a few products to someone who had turned down the opportunity. It turned out that it was the first time in his life that he had ever sold anything to anybody. His dream is to eventually build his network full time, because he is disillusioned with his present working environment in the medical profession. He finally realized that his entire future depended solely on his own efforts.

Although selling scares most people, there are people who love to sell. These people can produce fantastic personal volume. It is very important to know how to identify these people and welcome them into your organization because they could soon lose interest in this business if they were only encouraged to sponsor.

To summarize retail sales: make sure you use all the products yourself, then offer them to those people who are not interested in joining the business. It is as simple as that.

Duplication

Let us see what happens when duplication becomes part of the game.

In theory, suppose you sponsor six people who in turn sponsor six people, who will each sponsor six more people. Your network would then consist of 259 people, including yourself. If each person purchases and/or sells $100 worth of products, your total volume would be $25,900. You would be entitled to a performance bonus on that amount.

The figures noted above are only hypothetical. It will not necessarily work that way. Each person will not always sponsor six other people. Some will sponsor more, some less. However, what is important to remember is that duplication multiplies your personal efforts many times over.

In the long run, it is better to have 1,000 people whose volume would be $100 per month than to have 100 people who each would sell $1,000 per month. Remember what J. Paul Getty said: "It is better to receive 1 % of the results of the efforts of 100 people than 100 % of my own efforts".

A standard of performance for each person involved in the network is very important. In order for the business to function properly and to do well financially, each distributor should set personal minimum standards for himself. He should also supply his retail customers with products every month without fail.

a. **Support**

There is one aspect of the business that you must never neglect. Once you have sponsored someone, it is very important to spend as much time as possible with that person, to offer support and advice until he/she duplicates your efforts. Do not make the mistake of sponsoring someone and believing that he/she is good enough to manage on his/her own. Remember, you are the expert. Your distributor may be an expert in his field, but you are the specialist in this one.

There is a world of difference between sponsoring someone and having someone simply sign up. Sponsoring means helping a person believe in himself and in the network so that you grow together.

b.   Quitters

Some people will leave your organization even if you are the best sponsor in the world. This type of business, ironically, because it is accessible to a broad range of people, has developed its own natural selection process. It eliminates the individuals who are not ready to invest the necessary efforts, and those who are not used to teamwork. We must accept the fact that it is an integral part of the system.

C)   Make it stick together

In this business, it is important to develop close relationships with one another. I often use the expression "put glue" between your distributors so that your organization is held together with special ties that bind. This is why you will want to treat each distributor in your group, as if you had sponsored him or her personally. Moreover, if a distributor leaves the organization for whatever reason, you will have developed a relationship with the distributors downline. The best way to make it stick together is to hold counselling sessions once or twice a month in order to draw up plans with the serious ones. Ask the participants to bring their day planner and their organization chart. Discuss the challenges they are experiencing. These private sessions are the perfect time to discuss their dreams and goals. Remember, they are the embryo of your organization. Try to be creative and talk about new ideas, suggest innovative ways to have fun developing the network. Remember that this business succeeds with the perfect duplication process and that what you teach will in turn be taught to their distributors and so on.

At the counselling sessions, stress the importance of being loyal to, and appreciative of their line of sponsorship. Edify their upline; God knows they may not be perfect, but it does prove that if they could succeed, so can you! Always, remember that you can rely on your upline. Think of your upline as your lifeline. This is one of the most beneficial aspects of this whole concept.

Do not feel offended if your sponsor or an upline works closely with some of your distributors. The more they help them succeed, the more they help you succeed.

Create a family spirit within your group. Do not become too close or too intimate. Remember, familiarity can breed contempt. Just try to be the person that they would like to become. Set a good example.

Along the way you will realize that some people will disappoint you and others will surprise you. But never let any circumstances or anyone destroy your dreams.

Overall, you remain the most important person in your group. As long as you believe in the system and the products, you will ignore setbacks and keep on keeping on. What you really want and what you believe in will determine the price that you are willing to pay to make all your dreams come true.

Again, remember that what comes easy does not always have much value. So, pay the price with a smile and welcome freedom and financial independence for you and your family.

The flowers of tomorrow are in the seeds of today!

Chapter 7

The Commandments for Success

The burning desire

Considering the criteria for a successful business and the factors mentioned earlier, one must have a great deal of personal incentive to act and persevere. There is no one to tell you to get to work or to scare you by threatening you with your job. You do not have to report to anyone on a daily basis. There is no one to check on you to see if you are at work. You would be a very lucky person indeed, if in the beginning people asked you to join your business. You are the one who must provide the discipline and all the self-motivation. It must come from within. There is no other way.

In my case, I had a feeling deep in my soul, as far back as I could remember, that something special would happen to me. Why? Because I was searching, and I wanted it to happen. I had little formal education, and I knew that to be above average, I had to have my own business in order to be financially independent. Having no savings, I just could not see how I would ever start my own business. In the workforce since I was 12, I had learned that nothing came easily and that I had to pay the price for success. I was willing to do that, but I needed an opportunity. There is a saying that goes: "When opportunity knocks at their door, some people are in the back yard looking for a "four-leaf clover" or else they "complain about the noise". One has to recognize a golden opportunity, even if it is sometimes disguised in working clothes.

In 1967, when network marketing knocked at my door, the idea appealed to me right away even though this type of business was very new and had not yet made its mark.

I literally felt in love with the business. Mainly because, it was a business focusing on people more than anything else, and I love dealing with people. I knew that Henry Ford had a passion for automobiles, that Alexander Graham Bell had developed a passion for telephones, that the Wright brothers had a passion for airplanes. I was therefore convinced that my passion for people would eventually make me successful. I had a need, a burning desire and an inner drive to provide a better lifestyle for my family. I always had big dreams but unfortunately, only a small salary. This is what it was like:

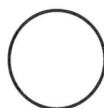

Furs
House
Cars
Trips
Boats
Savings
Education
Investments

DREAMS   INCOME

My parents and my friends had repeatedly tried to teach me to be realistic and to cut my dreams down to the size of my income. When I was introduced to network marketing, the negative teaching went out the window. I decided there and then to take my non-productive time and make it work for me. I was going to increase my income and make *ALL* of my dreams come true.

I invested everything I had and was into becoming a success. I did not just make an attempt to succeed, I was ready to do everything humanly and honestly possible to do so. When you give yourself completely to something and you really want to succeed, it is strange how everything seems to fall into place. Unfortunately, many people start a business on a "trying" basis, just to see if it will work out. If you limit your efforts to just trying, you give in to your doubts and you are doomed from the start. You throw in the towel at the first challenge or give up after the first failure.

To desire success is not enough; to want it is a good start. But it has to be a need if you want to achieve and maintain success. A burning desire nestled in your gut will help you climb mountains. A lukewarm desire keeps you inactive, glued to the TV set with a beer and potato chips, watching those behind the screen succeed. It will make us do anything to escape reality, the reality of failure.

Develop that burning desire. Show the people around you that you really mean business and that you, like a stamp, will stick to it until you reach your destination.

My recipe

People often tell me that my enthusiasm and my self-motivation seems so natural that they are difficult to imitate. I am asked how to acquire these traits.

What makes my wife and I have the energy and enthusiasm to stay anchored in our decision to succeed in life? OUR DREAMS.

There is nothing more electrifying than visualizing the objects of your desires. How many times have we imagined on our mental screen, boarding a plane with our family to go on a trip, or sitting in a new Mercedes at a dealership seeing the car as ours, or owning a new home, or building and completely furnishing our dream home, or trying on a magnificent fur coat that makes us look like a million dollars?

How many times in these last 28 years have we dreamed about things or events that gave us the incentive to hang on to it, to go on? We have lost count.

For some people dreams are just dreams but for others, dreams are the fuel that keeps the motor running. Some people devote entirely too much time learning HOW to do something, rather than finding out the reason WHY to do it. When we know WHY, we discover how.

A fool proof method

Let's take a brief look at our method of being successful with network marketing. I will divide it into two categories: basics you must do and how attitude affects your success.

Basics you must do

a) *Use all your products and services*

Whether you have access to a few products or services or to hundreds or even thousands of them, the first rule is definitely to be your own best customer.

It would be unthinkable to see a Ford dealer drive a Chrysler or to see the owner of a grocery store to buy from his competitor. You must use all the products and services that you distribute. Only by being a total consumer yourself, can you ever convince others to do the same. If you do not use your own products, others won't either. Your business is doomed from the start.

Convince them by setting an example, which is the best teaching method there is.

b) *Don't take anything personally*

When you begin in network marketing, you will realize that some of the people you want most to associate with in your business, do not share your interest. Some people, often family and friends will try to undermine you and try to make you feel small or cheap. Never take these refusals as personal attacks. In most cases, these people are not saying no to you, they are saying no to the opportunity, and no to their dreams and their future. It is their choice.

Besides, if they are not interested, that is *their* problem. You do not need that one particular person. You are looking for someone who has dreams and who wants to make them come true.

c) *Do not build alone*

This business gives you the opportunity to build a team: teamwork is the winner's secret. You are part of a team, even when you are the leader. A tyrant will push his people and say "Go". A real leader will say "Let's go!". It makes all the difference in the world especially when you consider that you will lead some day thousands of people.

You should also learn to make proper use of your upline. It is to your advantage. Always remember that there is someone above you who is eager to see you succeed. Find someone upline in whom you have the utmost faith, someone that you are very comfortable with. Ask that person to counsel you on how to become successful in the fastest way possible.

d) *Respect your line of sponsorship*

When you fill out the registration form to become a distributor, you are joining an organization originating directly from the company. By following the line of sponsorship or, if you prefer, the family tree, you will discover that any organization originates from someone who was sponsored by one of the founders of the company.

All the organizations are alike because they purchase their products from the company at wholesale prices, they get the same bonuses, and they abide by the principles of the parent company, which are based on honesty and integrity.

Many of these organizations have developed leaders who build their networks in different ways. The basic differences can be found in their philosophy and their network development strategies.

Although you are told on many occasions that this is a business based on sharing and love, it is not a good idea to go from one organization to the other to obtain what is called cross-line information. To begin with, this can create some confusion about the techniques that are being taught and also lead you to believe that you need another organization pattern to succeed. Your performance is in no way linked to your upline pattern. If you do not succeed, it is probably because you are not committed and do not apply the success pattern you are taught.

Try to perceive sponsorship as a copyright that forever belongs to the person who created the process. You will then realize that even though you may not have the ideal sponsor (is there such a thing?), you are still indebted to him. He approached you to introduce you to the marketing plan, to make you join and then to teach you the ropes. Therefore, he deserves your loyalty. This same principle applies to you and to your distributors once you become a sponsor.

In any serious network marketing organization, you cannot shift from one group to another unless you have been totally inactive for at least six months. However, I have discovered that if people transferred all the energy they use to criticize their line of sponsorship and invested it into building their own business, they would accomplish more, and could probably create miracles.

Throughout my many years in the business, I have seen very few cases, if any, where individuals actually changed from one line of sponsorship to another, and then became successful. I have also come to realize that distributors who do not succeed "because of their sponsor", (I do admit that there could be a legitimate challenge and the only solution they can see is to hide from reality rather than to solve the problem or go around it) will undoubtedly stumble again as soon as they face another challenge.

e) *Beware of scavengers*

From time to time, a new network marketing company with a plan "similar" to Amway will show up in the marketplace. The people who start these new companies will approach you and your distributors and say things such as "It's just like

Amway, only better" or they will try to make you join by saying: "Jump on the bandwagon. The company is just starting. It's the best time to join".

In a more subtle way, they may suggest: "You can add this business to your current business. It will help you" or "There is more money to be made in our network, and it is easier".

Some opportunists who are unable to build a business on their own from scratch, and who are really eager for instant success, will tend to recruit people that have been trained by another company. These people are scavengers. Fortunately, they will most likely take from you the people who are not succeeding in your network anyway.

Nonetheless, be alert and keep your eyes open because you can unknowingly be courted to accept and sell the products of other companies through your network. And all of a sudden, you will realize that your organization has different plans and different products. Consequently, everyone's efforts are diluted and so are the results, and in the end, you will lose your credibility.

Whenever I find a scavenger at one of my meetings, I simply inform him or her that he/she is not welcome. These people rarely succeed at anything. Except to create confusion.

Many years ago, a distributor from our group approached Françoise and I to ask us to join a new network company which sold a device designed to heat up your car engine by remote control. He told me that Amway only paid us pennies whereas his organization would make us earn dollars. I told him that I preferred to earn pennies forever rather than dollars temporarily and I boldly threw him out of my home. Before leaving, he threatened that he would lure away the best distributor in our group. He managed to lure away one Direct Distributor, who decided to beleive in his mirage and joined his organization. However, his success was short lived and he has gone bankrupt several times since.

Believe in the opportunity you choose with all your heart. Make sure that you have done everything humanly possible to make the business work before you look at something else. However, if you cannot succeed with this simple business, do not expect to accomplish miracles elsewhere.

f) *Keep your sense of humour*

"If we are not worth a laugh, we are not worth much." It is possible that friends and family may laugh at you. Expect them to. There are two kinds of people in this world, those who succeed and those who laugh at those who succeed.

When someone asks me what is the first thing that he should do in this business, I tell him to find a joker who will make fun of him... Thanks to my mother-in-law and my wife, I was saved.

Many people made fun of me. I have learned to laugh at these experiences, particularly when I laughed all the way to the bank. Whatever happens, keep on smiling and see the lighter side of life; it is better for your health and it will keep your enemies wondering.

g) *Keep your sight on the future*

It all starts with a dream, a thought. Everything in this world was created from a thought.

When someone starts a network marketing business, that person needs to concentrate on the results and not on the efforts. Since no major financial investment is required at first, it could become easy to procrastinate or think that it is too small a business to bother with, or that it requires too much time.

The difference between working for someone else and building a network is explained this way: a job requires permanent efforts for temporary income, while building a network requires temporary efforts for permanent income.

Join the parade. Do not watch it pass *you* by.

How attitude affects your success Attitude is everything

Be enthusiastic

The main ingredient for success is undoubtedly enthusiasm; that excitement felt at the beginning, in believing that your dreams can come true. Later on, the knowledge that you acquire will maintain the early excitement you felt.

It is imperative that you hang on to that enthusiam, through the bad as well as the good times. That is how we learn to grow and progress in life. Norman Vincent Peale, international well known author, believes that even an engineer needs 95 % enthusiasm and only 5 % knowledge to succeed.

Be persistent

There are people who never undertake anything because they are afraid to fail. So what? How many times do you think that most inventors failed before finally coming up with the one idea that worked, an idea that we all now take for granted? If Lindberg had been afraid to fail, would we travel by plane today? What if Graham Bell had been afraid to fail when he decided to improve communications? You cannot succeed if you are unwilling to accept potential failure. But then again, if used wisely, failures can become the stepping stones for you to climb higher.

"The easiest thing to do is quit. Any idiot can do that."

Unfortunately, there are people, who as soon as they face an obstacle, a challenge or a problem, come to a dead stop because they believe these things happen simply to baffle them or to make life complicated. We must understand that each situation in life helps shape our future and our character, that each blow is not meant to discourage us but to give us incentive to surpass ourselves to see how high we can bounce back when we have been knocked down. Only then will we understand that we are simply acquiring the necessary knowledge and experience we need to help others. We must channel our thoughts in a positive direction and concentrate on solutions. There is *always* a solution. There is night because there is day, black exists because there is white, and negative exists because there is positive and challenges exist because there are solutions. The solution may not always be immediately visible, but it *is* there. Become a possibility thinker.

During hard times, hang on extra tight to your dreams. Make a special effort to concentrate on your goals, read and listen to motivational material, talk with your sponsor to seek help, encouragement and love.

I like to hang on to some inspiring words of wisdom that relate to me personally. I would like to share one with you which has helped me considerably.

Press on

"Nothing in the world can take the place of persistence.

TALENT WILL NOT: Nothing is more common than unsuccessful men with talent.

GENIUS WILL NOT: Unrewarded genius is almost a proverb.

EDUCATION WILL NOT: The world is full of educated derelicts.

Persistence and determination alone are omnipotent.

Be consistent

The secret in this business is that there is no secret. The key though is to do the same things, over and over again. You must explain the marketing plan, over and over again patiently. Regardless of the results you get. But your line of sponsorship will teach you the techniques to get positive results. Perhaps one day you may end up sponsoring the one person who will break all records.

Be positive

To reach the higher levels of success, you must be very selective of what you store on the diskette of your subconscious. You must carefully and deliberately screen every piece of material that you allow into it. We all tend to believe that our conscious side controls. It does, in the end, but what does it feed on? It feeds on what has accumulated in our subconscious. Reading the daily newspaper, listening to the evening news before falling asleep, or listening to gossip cannot generate a positive attitude and create the enthusiasm needed to build and succeed.

Take great care of what enters into your mind and you will generate a much healthier response from both your mind and your body.

For many years, I posted this sentence by the front door of my home: "If you cannot be positive here, go be negative somewhere else." Do not let your friends' or your family's negative attitude discourage you. Some will try to destroy your dreams by saying: "It will never work, it's too late, it's old news, what makes you think you can succeed?" Let them talk and remember, SUCCESS IS REVENGE.

Gain strength from the success stories of people that you hear at meetings or on tapes. Read books that will help you gain self-confidence, inspire personal motivation and generate an extraordinary positive mental attitude, which will shield you against all failures.

Commit yourself 100 %

Someone once told me: "André, I wouldn't like to work as hard as you do." I quickly replied: "And I certainly don't want to work as long as you will have to."

Every winner and every champion began as a novice. In reality, the greatest risk of all is that of letting life control your destiny. If there is a fee to pay at the door of success then, that price must be total commitment. The greatest motivation is telling yourself that you will do *whatever* it takes to succeed, no matter what.

You have to be convinced at 200 % to commit 100 %. Make things happen. Success will not just fall on your lap. You always have to be on the lookout for it.

Be patient

At the beginning of this book, I mentioned that you need a vision to succeed: a vision of the future. A farmer never sells his farm in the winter time. He knows that if he plants seeds in the spring, there will be crops in the fall. He does not expect a green garden the next day nor the week after. During the dormant period he lets the land germinate and confidently waits for mother nature to help him out again. Life has its cycles, and so does your business.

You have to put in several consecutive months of constant efforts to harvest what you have sowed.

The victory cup goes to the person who believes that he or she deserves it.

Developing a winning attitude is not a coincidence. It is a choice. The highest reward of hard work is not what it allows you to obtain but what it allows you to become.

Where will you be five years from now? Time flies. You need to ask yourself that question. One thing is definitely sure. You will be five years older. But will you be five years happier, five years more satisfied, five years more accomplished thanks to your vision and your decision?

Devote your life

Here is an anecdote that I read somewhere. Following an extraordinary performance by a musician, a woman introduces herself to the musician and says, "I would give my life to play as well as you do". He replied, "That is exactly what I have done."

Do not look for motivation other than within yourself, within your own desires. IT IS ALREADY INSIDE YOU! IN YOUR DREAMS!

Always think big

People are unreasonable, illogical and egotistical: *Love them anyway.*

If you lend a helping hand, they will accuse you of being selfish and of having other motives: *Give a helping hand anyway.*

When you succeed, you will gain untrue friends and gain enemies: *Give all you have to succeed anyway.*

Honesty and truthfulness will lead you nowhere; they make you vulnerable: *Be honest and truthful anyway.*

People favour the unlucky but follow the lucky: *Fight for the unlucky anyway.*

What can be built in many days can be destroyed in one night: *Build it anyway.*

People really need help but they attack you when you try to help: *Help them anyway.*

Give the world the best part of yourself and it will hit you in the face: *Give the world the best of yourself anyway.*

Continue to move forward and to think big.

Author unknown

Chapter 8

Two Invitations

An invitation to never quit

Now that you have read this book, if you already belong to an organization or if you are just developing your own network, I invite you to give it all you've got, and don't be afraid to seek out the help you need to achieve the success you want. There is someone in your line of sponsorship who wants you to succeed, as much as you do. Contact this person. It is important to seek advice from your upline, *providing they are growing and involved in the action*. Never hesitate to contact your Direct Distributor. He is your best "tool" in building your business.

Here is a message that Françoise and I, as active distributors in network marketing, would like to dedicate to you. Read it again on those days when you feel like quitting.

May it comfort you and keep you on the road to success.

TO YOU

If at times you fall, pick yourself up again and get going faster than ever.

Know that failure is part of life and that it shows a will to live and to risk. It brings you closer to your ideals.

Therefore, live your life by telling yourself that your dreams will come true one at a time, and that each minute, each hour and each day that goes by invariably leads you closer to your destiny, the one you have chosen. Each day is rich with promises, and it helps you appreciate new experiences you never had before and do things you never would have done, had it not been for your dreams. Live for today in happiness and enthusiasm.

Live as if your dreams had become realities and know that your attitude creates your successes or your failures. You must intensely think about your dreams, in order for them to come true. Your imagination is the key to your future. It is a choice and a decision that you make on your own. It may not always be easy but that does not mean that your dreams cannot become reality. You must persevere.

With each day that goes by, take the time to visualize on the screen of your mind the images and scenes of your dreams and of your goals. Imagine them very precisely and in great detail and say: I can, I want, I am, I bless these dreams and I deserve to live a life filled with the best it contains. Amen.

Never choose to set your dreams aside, because it is your life itself that you would chose to set aside. Get into action and stay in action. Consequently, you will act in such a way that every instant, every moment of your life will be beneficial to you. The minutes of your life are already counted. Each part of every minute is more precious than the most precious of jewels because it allows you to become what YOU want to be, to develop your full potential, to move in the direction YOU have chosen while the diamond, even the purest of diamonds will always remain just a diamond, whereas YOU, can and will rise towards the highest peaks, if that is what you choose.

Of all your assets, the greatest and most precious one is your enthusiasm. Be enthusiastic towards life, but more importantly towards yourself. YOU. There is so much to say about YOU that it is hard to know where to start. But, to begin with, the fact is that YOU must love yourself. How can other people love you if you don't love yourself? Who else is there but you? To be your own best friend is the best thing you can do for yourself and, I would even say, for humanity. What would humanity be if it consisted only of individuals who did not like themselves, who underestimated themselves, who put themselves down? Would you like to live on a planet devoid of love and enthusiasm? It all starts in yourself, within yourself. Do you know that, thanks to you, the world can be a great place to live? Leave YOUR mark, your imprints forever.

The promises that you make to yourself are more important than those you make to others because, although you must not cheat others, it is even more important to be able to rely on yourself. Therefore, respect the promises you make to yourself, because breaking such a promise is like insulting God, your Creator. Like it or not, and believe it or not, you are His child. Once you are committed, prepare yourself to act accordingly and to harvest the fruits you sowed.

To succeed is to live tenfold, adapting to the great dimensions of the world.

To succeed is to participate both in spirit and in action in the destiny of mankind.

With all our love

André and Françoise Blanchard

A Personal Invitation

If you are not yet part of a marketing network, I invite you to build your financial independence through the Amway opportunity.

Your dreams can become realities. Nobody will tell you that it will be easy and you will never hear of any way this organization will make you rich without working. However, you will be encouraged to follow your dreams, to build for tomorrow and to work for a better life for yourself and your family.

After all, you have absolutely nothing to lose: TAKE THE RISK!

To Risk
by Rudyard Kipling

To laugh is to risk appearing the fool; to weep is to risk appearing sentimental.

To reach out for another is to risk involvement.

To expose feelings is to risk exposing your true self; to place your ideas, your dreams before the crowd, is to risk loss; to love is to risk not being loved in return.

To live is to risk dying. To hope is to risk despair. To try at all is to risk failure.

But risk we must — because the greatest hazard in life is to risk nothing. The person who risks nothing does nothing... has nothing... is20nothing...

He may avoid suffering — but he simply cannot learn, feel, change, grow, love or live. Chained by his servitudes, he is a slave. He has forfeited freedom.

Only the person who risks, can be called free.

Network Marketing Lexicon

Upline:

Person above in the line of sponsorship

Down-Line:

Person below in the line of sponsorship.

Network Marketing:

See explanation in Chapter 2: *Network Marketing*

Sponsor:

Person who brings you into the network.

Pattern for success:

Precise and systematic work method which includes the actions that will ultimately lead a person to the achievement of his goals and of the organization's goals.

imprimerie gagné ltée

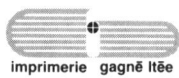

IMPRIMÉ AU CANADA